Understanding

A Gateway into reading the Bible for new Christians

Cyril A Sansum

RB
Rossendale Books

Published by Lulu Enterprises Inc.
3101 Hillsborough Street
Suite 210
Raleigh, NC 27607-5436
United States of America

Published in paperback 2017
Category: Christianity
Copyright C. A. Sansum © 2017
ISBN : 978-0-244-34198-5

All rights reserved, Copyright under the Berne Copyright Convention and Pan American Convention. No part of this book may be reproduced, stored in a retrieval system, or transmitted in any form or by any means, electronic, mechanical, photocopying, recording or otherwise, without prior permission of the author. The author's moral rights have been asserted

Contents

INTRODUCTION 9

PART ONE - PROPHETS OF THE OLD TESTAMENT 13
    Chapter One - Noah to Ephraim 15
        Noah 15
        Melchizedek 17
        Abraham 17
        Isaac 24
        Jacob 26
        Joseph 39
        Ephraim 45
    Chapter Two - Moses to Samuel 46
        Moses 46
        Aaron 52
        Miriam 55
        Joshua 57
        Deborah 63
        Gideon 65
        Samuel 70
    Chapter Three - Saul to Iddo 75
        Saul 75
        Nathan 78
        Gad 79
        Shemaiah 79
        Iddo 80
    Chapter Four - Prophets of Israel: Alijah to Oded 83
        Alijah 83
        Micaiah 83
        Hosea 85
        Amos 88
        Jonah 91
        Elijah 96
        Elisha 104
        Oded 108

Chapter Five - Prophets of Judah: Hanani to Habakkuk 109
- Hanani 109
- Jehu 109
- Jahaziel 110
- Eliezer 110
- Obadiah 111
- Jahaziel 112
- Joel 112
- Amoz 113
- Isaiah 113
- Micah 116
- Nahum 117
- Neriah 120
- Urijah 120
- Jeremiah 120
- Zephaniah 127
- Habakkuk 130

Chapter Six - The Captive Prophets: Daniel to Seraiah 132
- Daniel 132
- Ezekiel 156
- Mordecai 159
- Seraiah 160

Chapter Seven - Prophets of the Return: Ezra to Zechariah 162
- Ezra 162
- Haggai 164
- Malachi 166
- Nehemiah 167
- Zechariah 169

Conclusion 171

PART TWO - THE NEW TESTAMENT 175
The Twelve Disciples 176
- Peter 177
- Andrew 182
- James the Elder 184
- John the Apostle 185
- Bartholomew 187

  James the Lesser 188
  Judas Escariot 189
  Jude 191
  Philip 191
  Simon the Zealot 192
  Thomas 193
  Matthew 194
 Acts 196
St Paul 204
Last words - The Beginning 214

PART THREE - DROWNING IN THE HOLY SPIRIT 215

 Drowning in the Holy Spirit 216
 A Gift of Love 217
 God's anger 218
 My Father in Heaven 219
 Thank you 220
 This one's for you 221
 Searching for the star 223
 A Lesson in Biology 224
 Have you heard 226
 Fruits of the Spirit - Patience 227
 Footprints 229
 A Child of God 231
 Left Behind - 1 Thessalonians 4:16-17 232
 Faith 234
 The Promise of God - Sealed with the blood of Jesus 236
 Broken Chains 237
 A Letter to God 238
 Walking with God 239
 Psalm 151 240

Dedication

I Dedicate this book to my Loving wife Diane, who has supported me through my Journey through my Christian life.

INTRODUCTION

When we first give our lives to God, we then want to learn all about him. The natural place to do our research is the Holy Bible.

Now Which Bible will you chose? The choice of Bible is a minefield, as there are so many to choose from.

In our home we have: The King James Bible, The Good News Bible, The New International Bible, A Youth Bible and we even have a Cockney Bible.

Go to a Christian book shop and read a selection of Bibles before buying your own personal Bible.

Next step, where do you start to read?

The Bible is divided into two parts, the Old Testament, which contains 39 Books. It covers a period of 2000 years before the birth of Jesus. The New Testament contains 27 books. These were written after the death of Jesus.

Do you start at the Beginning? With the Book of Genesis, the start of the creation of the world, the beginning of mankind? Or start at the birth of Jesus at the book of Matthew?

We may be familiar with his birth as it is celebrated at Christmas every December. Or we can select parts which we are familiar with - such as Daniel and the Lions, Samson fighting the Philistines, The Jews escaping from Egypt or Jesus and the Miracles he performed.

When I first had a Bible I started at the beginning, but it was hard to read. So I switched to reading the bits which I know about like Samson and Daniel. The problem with this method is that we miss so many important parts. For example, I was reading about Daniel and the lions and his friends who were put in the furnace (this is covered in the first 6 chapters of Daniel). But it is the chapters that come after Daniel has his visions, which are so important to know.

Also, lots of times the birth and death of Jesus are forecast in the Old Testament.

This is a beginner's book, which is designed to help new Christians to read the Bible.

- ❖ First you will read about the Old Testament prophets. These men and women were very brave and were often killed serving God.

- ❖ Then the book moves to the New Testament and tells us about the 12 Disciples of Jesus. Also you will learn about St Paul, who was maybe the Apostle who spread the Good News the furthest.

- ❖ You will also look at the Book of Acts. Where Gentiles were also given the Good News.

- ❖ Jesus did not need any help as he is God, but I believe he wanted people to travel with him as witnesses, these were his disciples.

- ❖ Then after his Death on the Cross and his Resurrection, they would go throughout the world spreading the Good News.

Who were the disciples? They were just ordinary people like you and me, just going about their lives. Some were married but when Jesus said "Follow me" they stopped what they were doing and followed him.

This book is not going to explain all that is written in the Bible. It is written for the new Christian, as an easy Gateway to the Bible.

It's a taster hoping you will want to read more.

I will now stop and leave you to start your journey at the beginning of time.

PART ONE - PROPHETS OF THE OLD TESTAMENT

Prophets are men and women that have been clearly called or chosen by God. Some are defined as Major Prophets, others are defined as Minor Prophets.

The prophets mentioned in this book have clearly been defined as prophets, either by explicit statement or strong contextual implication.

In Roman Catholicism, prophets are recognised as having received either public or private revelations. Public revelations is part of "deposit of faith", which refers to the entire revelation of Jesus Christ passed to successive generations in the forms of sacred traditions.

The second list consists of those individuals who are recorded as having had a visionary or prophetic experience, but without a history of any major or consistent prophetic calling.

The Old Testament period can be divided into four equal sections of about 500 years each.

Each period has a key event, a prominent event and a type of leadership. In the first period the patriarchs led Israel: Abraham, Isaac, Jacob and Joseph. In the second period Israel was led by Prophets, from Moses to Samuel. In the third period they were led by princes (Kings), from Saul to

Zedekiah. In the last period we see the priests take the lead, from Joshua to Caiaphas in the time of Christ.

Names of the prophets in this book

Noah   Jonah   Elijah   Elisha   Hanani
Melchizedek   Jehu   Oded   Obadiah   Jahaziel
Abraham   Eliezer   Isaiah   Joel   Amoz   Nahum
Isaac   Micah   Jeremiah   Neriah   Urijah
Zephaniah   Jacob   Habakkuk   Joseph   Daniel
Ezekiel   Mordecai   Ephraim   Moses   Seraiah
Ezra   Haggai   Aaron   Malachi   Nehemiah
Miriam   Joshua   Zechariah   Iddo   Deborah
Gideon   Hosea   Micaiah   Samuel   Saul
Alijah   Shemiah   Nathan   Gad   Amos

Chapter One - Noah to Ephraim

Noah

Noah's father was Lamech, his mother is unknown.

When Noah was 500 years old, Shem, Ham and Japeth were born.

Genesis 6-9 covers the story of the flood.

Mankind was becoming so evil, that God had decided to destroy the Earth.

God told Noah to build an Arc to hold certain animals and his family.

God guaranteed the continued existence of life under the promise that he would never send another flood.

After the flood Noah offered burnt offerings to God.

God blessed Noah and his sons and said to them, Be fruitful, and multiply.

God said "between every living creature that is with you, for perpetual generations, I give you the Noahic covenant or the rainbow covenant".

Noah died 350 years after the flood at the age of 950.

Little is known about Noah.

One thing is sure, God trusted this man. He asked Noah to build an Arc (Big Boat) on land and wait until he sent a storm.

At the Beginning of the Bible God said that he had made the world and he was happy with it.

Now God had decided that man was so sinful that he had decided to destroy mankind and start again.

So God told Noah to build this Arc. Everybody thought he was a bit mad but he and his sons built the Arc and took the animals on board as God commanded.

God had chosen well here.

A good man who would always obey God.

I am sure that we will all agree Noah was a good man.

But after the flood, Noah planted a vineyard and when the grapes grew he made wine. Then he got drunk and was naked.

One of his sons Ham found him drunk and naked so he called two of his brothers.

When Noah woke up, he realised what had happened and cursed Ham and his brothers.

So maybe even Noah had some faults

Melchizedek

Melchizedek, is mentioned twice in the Hebrew Bible, the first in Genesis and the second in Psalms.

Genesis 14

The story of Genesis 14 is part of the larger story telling how Abram returns from defeating King Chedorlaomer and meets with Bera the King of Sodom, at which point Melchizedek King of Salem brought out bread and wine: and he was (is) the priest of the most High God. And he blessed him, and said, "Blessed be Abram to the most High God, possessor of Heaven and Earth, and blessed be the most High God, which hath delivered thine enemies into thy hands". And he gave him tithe from all. (Genesis 14:18-20).

Psalm 110

The second and final Hebrew mention of Melchizedek is in Psalm 110:4. The Lord hath sworn, and will not repent: "Thou art a priest for ever after the manner of Melchizedeh".

Abraham

Let's have a look at Abraham (Genesis 20: 7).

Abraham (originally named Abram), is called by God to leave the house of his father Terah and settle in the land originally given to Canaan. Canaan was at the time occupied by Canaanites which is an ethnic description for the various indigenous people, both settled and nomadic groups, throughout the region known as Canaan.

Abram's Origins

Terah his father, The Ninth in decent from Noah, had three sons: Abram, Nahor, and Haran.

Lot was the son of Haran.

Abram married Sarai, who was barren.

Terah, with Abram, Sarai, and Lot then departed for Canaan, but settled in a place named Haran, where Terah died at the age of 205.

(Genesis 11:27-32).

God told Abram to leave his country and family and go to a land that he would show him, and promised to make him a great nation, bless him, make his name great, bless them that blessed him, and curse those who may curse him. (Genesis 12:1-3)

Abram was 75 years old when he left Haran with his wife Sarai, his nephew Lot, and the substance and souls that they had acquired, and travelled to Shecham in Canaan. (Genesis 12: 4-6).

There was severe famine in the land of Canaan, so that Abram and Lot and their households, travelled south to Egypt.

On the way Abram told his wife Sarai to say that she was his sister, so that the Egyptians would not kill him. (Genesis 12:10-13)

A true man of God but why did he lie to the Egyptians saying his wife was his sister. At times we all lie to protect ourselves. What I see is there is hope for all of us.

When they arrived in Egypt, the Pharaoh's officials praised Sarai's beauty to the Pharaoh, and took her into his palace, and Abram was given lots of food and men and maid servants.

However God afflicted Pharaoh and his household with great plagues, for which he tried to find the reason (Genesis 12; 14-17).

Upon discovering that Sarai was a married woman, Pharaoh demanded that they and their household leave immediately, with all their goods.

When they arrived back to the Bethel and Hai area, Abram's and Lot's herds occupied the same pastures.

Abram graciously suggested that Lot choose a separate area, either on the left or on the right.

But Lot chose to go east to the plain of Jordan where the land was well watered everywhere as far as Zoar, and he dwelt in the city of Sodom.

Abram went south to Hebron and settled in the plains of Mamre, where he built another altar to worship God (Genesis 13; 1-18).

Later, after a confrontation between Abram and the Elamites, the voice of the Lord came to Abram in a vision and repeated the promise of the land and descendants as numerous as the stars.

Abram and Sarai tried to make sense of how he would become a progenitor of nations since after 10 years of living in Canaan, no child had been born.

Sarai then offered her Egyptian handmaiden, Hagar, for Abram to consort with so that he may have a child by her, as his wife.

After Hagar found she was pregnant, she began to despise her mistress, Sarai.

Therefore, Sarai mistreated Hagar, and Hagar fled away.

As she fled an Angel spoke with Hagar at the fountain on the way to Shur. He instructed her to return and that her son would be "a wild ass of a man: his hand shall be against every man, and every man's against him: and he shall dwell in the face of all his brethren.

"She was told to call her son Ishmael, Hagar then called God who spoke to her". Elroi -*Thou God seest me*. From that day the well was called Beer-Lahai-roi, ("the well of him that liveth and seeth me").

Abram was 86 years old when Ishmael was born.

Thirteen years later, when Abram was 99 years old, God declared Abrams new name "Abraham" a father of many nations

(Genesis 17; 5)

God also declared Sarai to be called Sarah.

Then God declared that he would give them a son.

Abraham laughed and said how can a man of a hundred years and a woman of ninety years bear a baby?

Some time after, during the heat of the day, Abraham had been sitting at the entrance of his tent. He looked up and saw three men in the presence of God. He ran and bowed to welcome them, Abraham then offered to wash their hands and feet and fetch them food.

One of the visitors told Abraham that when he returns next year, Sarah would have a son. Sarah overheard and laughed at the thought of a woman her age having a baby.

The visitor enquired why Sarah was laughing at the idea of bearing a child at her age, as nothing is too hard for God.

After eating, Abraham and the three visitors got up. They walked over to the peak that overlooked the cities of the plain to discuss the fate of Sodom and Gomorrah for their detestable sins that were so great, it moved God into action. Because Abraham's nephew was living in Sodom, God revealed plans to confirm and judge these cities. At this point, the two other visitors left for Sodom. Then Abraham turned to God and pleaded with him that "if there were at least ten righteous men found in the city, would not God spare the city?" for the sake of ten righteous people, God declared that he would not destroy the city if 10 righteous men were found, (Genesis 18: 17-33).

When the two visitors got to Sodom to conduct their report, they planned on staying in the city square. However, Abraham's nephew, Lot, met with them and insisted that these two 'men' stay at his house for the night. A group of men came to Lot's house and demanded that the two guests were given to them.

Lot objected and offered his two daughters who had not known men. They refused that offer and tried to break down his door.

Early the next morning, Abraham went to the place where he stood before God. He "looked out towards Sodom and Gomorrah" and saw what had become of the cities of the plain, where not even ten righteous people could be found.

Birth of Isaac

As it had been foretold the previous year, Sarah became pregnant and gave birth to a son, on the first anniversary of the covenant of circumcision. Abraham was one hundred years old when his son, who he named Isaac, was born.

Ishmael was fourteen years old when Abraham's son Isaac was born to a different mother, Sarah. Sarah had finally given birth to her own child, even though she had passed her child bearing period. When she found Ishmael teasing Isaac, she told Abraham to send both Ishmael and Hagar away.

Abraham was distressed by his wife's words and sought the advice of God. God told Abraham not to be distressed but to do what his wife commanded. God reassured Abraham that "in Isaac shall seed be called to thee" (Genesis 21:12)

At some point in Isaac's youth, Abraham was commanded by God to offer his son up as a Sacrifice in the land of Moriah. The Patriarch travelled three days until he came to the mount that God told him to.

He commanded his servants to remain while he and Isaac proceeded alone into the mount. Isaac carried the Wood upon which he would be sacrificed. Along the way, Isaac asked his father where the animal for the burnt offering was, to which Abraham replied "God will provide a lamb for a burnt offering" Just as Abraham was about to sacrifice his son, he was interrupted by the angel of the Lord, and he saw behind him a "ram caught in a thicket by the horns", which he sacrificed instead of his son.

For his obedience he received another promise of numerous descendants and abundant prosperity.

Abraham lived for 175 years.

Abraham was clearly a man of God.

God had promised to make his descendants as numerous as the stars.

Isaac

Isaac, was the second son of Abram, the only son Abram had with his wife Sarah, and the father of Jacob and Esau. According to Genesis, Abram was 100 years old when Isaac was born, and Sarah was past 90. Isaac was born about 1700 BC.

Isaac was one of the three patriarchs of the Israelites.

Isaac was the only biblical Patriarch whose name was not changed, and the only one who did not move out of Canaan.

He died when he was 180 years old.

At some point in Isaac's youth (some people believe it was while Isaac was in his thirties, don't forget to people who live as long as Isaac did, thirty odd years is in their youth. Isaac's grandfather, for example, lived to 205, his father Abraham lived to 175).

His father Abraham brought him to Mount Moriah. At God's command, Abraham was to build a sacrificial altar and sacrifice his son Isaac upon it. After he had bound his son to the altar and drawn his knife to kill him, at the very last moment an Angel of the Lord prevented Abraham from proceeding. Rather, he was directed to sacrifice a Ram which had got stuck in a bush. This event was a test of Abraham's faith in God.

Family life

When Isaac was 40, Abraham sent Eliezer, his steward, into Mesopotamia to find a wife for Isaac, from his nephew Bethuel's family. Eliezer chose the Aramean Rebekah for Isaac.

After many years of marriage to Isaac, Rebekah had still not given birth to a child and was believed to be barren. Isaac prayed for her and she conceived. Rebekah gave birth to twin boys, Esau and Jacob. Isaac was 60 years old when his two sons were born. Isaac favoured Esau, and Rebekah favoured Jacob.

Isaac is Unique among the Patriarchs for remaining faithful to his wife, and not having concubines.

Migration

At the age of 75, Isaac moved to Beer-Iahai-roi after his father died. When the land experienced famine, he moved to the Philistine land of Gerar where his father once lived. This land was still under the control of King Abimelech as it was in the days of Abraham. Like his father, Isaac also deceived Abimelech about his wife and also got into the well-digging business. He had gone back to all of the wells that his father dug and saw that they were all stopped up with earth. The Philistines did this after Abraham died. So, Isaac unearthed them and begun to dig for more wells all the way to Beersheba, where he made a pact with Abimelech, just as in the days of his father.

There was a dispute between Esau and Jacob about their birth right (you can read about this in the section about Jacob.).

Jacob was eventually reconciled with his twin brother Esau, then they buried Isaac in Hebron.

Jacob

Jacob was later given the name Israel. He was the son of Isaac and Rebecca, the grandson of Abraham.

Jacob had 12 sons and a daughter named Dinah. Jacobs 12 sons named in Genesis, became the progenitors of the "Tribes of Israel".

As a result of a severe drought in Canaan, Jacob and his sons moved to Egypt at the time when his son Joseph was viceroy.

After 17 years in Egypt, Jacob died and Joseph carried Jacob's remains to the land of Canaan, and gave him a stately burial in the same cave of Machpelah as were buried Abraham, Sarah, Isaac, Rebecca, and Jacob's wife, Leah.

Jacob is mentioned in a number of sacred scriptures, including the Hebrew Bible and the New Testament. His original name Ya'akov is sometimes explained as having meant "holder of the heel" because he was born holding his twin Brother Esau's heel, and eventually supplanted Esau in obtaining their father's blessing.

Jacob lived for 147 years.

The Biblical account of the life of Jacob is found in the Book of Genesis, chapters 25-50.

Genesis 25: 29-34 tells the account of Esau selling his birth right to Jacob. This passage tells that Esau, returning hungry from the fields, begging Jacob to give him some of the stew that Jacob had just made.

Jacob offered to give Esau a bowl of the stew in exchange for his birth right, to which Esau agreed.

As Isaac grew old, he became blind and was uncertain when he would die, so he decided to bestow Esau's birth right upon him.

He requested that Esau go out to the fields with his weapons and to kill a deer. Isaac then requested that Esau made a meal for him out of the Venison, according to the way he enjoyed it the most, so that he could eat it and bless Esau.

Rebecca overheard this conversation. It's suggested that she realized prophetically that Isaac's blessings would go to Jacob, since she was told before the twin's birth that the older son would serve the younger.

She quickly ordered Jacob to bring her two kid goats from the flock so that he could take Esau's place in serving Isaac and receiving his blessing. Jacob protested that his father would recognize their deception since Esau was hairy and he himself was smooth-skinned. He feared his father would curse him as soon as he felt him, but Rebecca offered to take the curse herself, then insisting that Jacob obey her. Jacob did as his mother instructed and. when he returned with the kids, Rebecca made the savoury meat that Isaac loved. Before she sent Jacob to his father, she dressed him in Esau's clothes and laid goatskins on his arms and neck to simulate hairy skin.

Disguised as Esau, Jacob entered Isaac's room. Surprised that Esau was back so soon, Isaac asked how it could be that the hunt went so quickly. Jacob responded, "Because the LORD your God brought it to me" Rashi, in Genesis 27:21.

Isaac's suspicions were aroused even more, because Esau never used the personal name of God. Isaac demanded that Jacob come close so he could feel him, but the goatskins felt just like Esau's hairy skin. Confused, Isaac exclaimed, "The voice is Jacob's voice, but the hands are the hands of Esau!" Genesis 27:22.

Still trying to get at the truth, Isaac asked him directly, "Art thou my very son Esau?" and Jacob answered simply, "I Am "Isaac proceeded to eat the food and to drink the wine that Jacob gave him, and then told him to come close and kiss him. As Jacob kissed his father, Isaac smelled the clothes which belonged to Esau and finally accepted that the person in front of him was Esau. Isaac then blessed Jacob with the Blessing that was meant for Esau, Genesis 27:28-29 states Isaac's blessings: "therefore God give thee of the dew of heavens, and the fatness of the earth, and plenty of corn and wine: Let people serve thee: be Lord over my brethren, and let thy mother's sons bow down to thee: cursed be every one that cursed thee, and blessed be the blessed thee."

Jacob had scarcely left the room when Esau returned from the hunt to prepare his game and receive the blessings. The realization that he had been deceived shocked Isaac, yet he acknowledged that Jacob had received the blessings by adding, "Indeed, he will be blessed!"

Esau was heartbroken by the deception and begged for his own blessing.

Having made Jacob a ruler over his brothers, Isaac could only promise, "by my sword you shall live, but your brother you shall serve; yet it shall be that when you are aggrieved, you may cast off his yoke from upon your neck".

Although Esau sold Jacob his own birth right, Esau still hated Jacob for receiving his blessing from his father.

He vowed to kill Jacob as soon as Isaac died.

When Rebecca heard about this, she told Jacob to travel to her brother Laban's house in Haran, until Esau's anger had cooled.

Jacob's ladder

Near Luz en route to Haran, Jacob experienced a vision of a ladder, reaching up to heaven with angels going up and down, commonly referred to as "Jacobs Ladder". He heard the voice of God, who repeated many of the blessings upon him, coming from the top of the ladder.

According to Rashi, the ladder signified the exiles that the Jewish people would suffer before the coming of the Jewish messiah: the Angels that represented the exiles of Babylonia, Persia, and Greece each climbed up a certain number of steps, paralleling the years of the exile, before they "fell down", but the angel representing the last exile, that of Edom, kept climbing higher and higher into the clouds. Jacob feared that his descendants would never be free of Esau's domination, but God assured him that at the End of Days, Edom too would come falling down.

In the morning, Jacob woke up and then continued on his way to Haran, after naming the place where he had spent the night "Bethel", "Gods house".

Jacobs Marriages

Arriving in Haran, Jacob saw a well where shepherds were gathering their flocks to water them and met Laban's younger daughter, Rachel, Jacob's first cousin; she was working as a shepherdess. He loved her immediately, and after a month with his relatives, asked for her hand in marriage in return for working seven years for Laban the Aramean. Laban agreed to the arrangement. These seven years seemed to Jacob "but a few days, for the love he had for her", but when they were complete and he asked for his wife, Laban deceived Jacob by switching Rachel's older sister, Leah, as the veiled bride.

(There was a lot of crafty people about then and also now).

In the morning, when the truth was known, Laban justified his action, saying that in his country it was unheard of to give a younger daughter before the older. However, he agreed to give Rachel in marriage as well if Jacob would work another seven years. After the week of wedding celebrations with Leah, Jacob married Rachel, and he continued to work for Laban for another seven years.

Jacob loved Rachel more than Leah, and Leah felt hated. God opened Leah's womb and she gave birth to four sons rapidly: Reuben, Simeon, Levi, and Judah. Rachel, however, remained barren. Following the example of Sarah, who gave her handmaid to Abraham after years of infertility, Rachel gave Jacob her handmaid, Bilhah, in Marriage so that Rachel could raise children through her. Bilhah gave birth to Dan and Naphtali. Seeing that she had left off childbearing temporarily, Leah then gave her handmaid Zilpah to Jacob in marriage so that Leah could raise more children through her.

Zilpah gave birth to Gad and Asher. (According to The Testaments of the Patriarchs, Testament of Naphtali, Chapter 1, lines 9-12, Bilhah and Zilhah were daughters of Rotheus and Euna, servants of laban.)

Afterwards, Leah became fertile again and gave birth to Issachar, Zebulun, and Dinah, Jacob's first and only daughter. God remembered Rachel, who gave birth to Joseph and Benjamin.

The Journey back to Canaan

As Jacob neared the land of Canaan, he sent messengers ahead to his brother Esau. They returned with the news that Esau was coming to meet Jacob with an army of over 400 men. With great worry, Jacob prepared for the worst. He spent a lot of time praying to God, then sent on before him a tribute of flocks and herds to Esau, "a present to my Lord Esau from thy servant Jacob".

Then Jacob took his family and flocks across the ford Jabbok by night, then re crossed back to send over his possessions, being left alone in communion with God. There, a mysterious being appeared ("man", Genesis 32: 24, 28, or "God" Genesis 32:28, 30,) and the two wrestled until daybreak. When the being saw he did not overpower Jacob, he touched Jacob on the sinew of his thigh and, as a result, Jacob developed a limp (Genesis 32: 31). Because of this, "to this day the people of Israel do not eat the sinew of the thigh that is on the hip socket"

Jacob then demanded a blessing, and the being declared in Genesis 32: 28 that, from then on, Jacob would be called Israel, meaning "one that struggled with the divine angel".

Jacob asked the being's name, but he refused to answer.

After Joseph was born, Jacob decided to return to his parents. Laban the Aramean was reluctant to release him, as God had blessed his flock on account of Jacob. Laban asked what he could pay Jacob. Jacob suggested that all the spotted, speckled, and brown goats and sheep of Laban's flock, at any given moment, would be his wages. Jacob placed peeled rods of poplar, hazel, and Chestnut within the flocks' watering holes or troughs, an action he later attributes to a dream.

As time passed, Laban's sons noticed that Jacob was taking the better part of their flocks, and so Laban's friendly attitude changed to Jacob. God told Jacob that he should leave, which he and his wives and children did without informing Laban. Before they left, Rachel stole the teraphim, considered to be household idols, from Laban's house.

In rage, Laban chased after Jacob. The night before he caught up with him, God appeared to Laban in a dream and warned him not to say anything good or bad to Jacob. When the two met, Laban played the part of the injured father in law, demanding his teraphim back. Knowing nothing about Rachel's theft, Jacob told Laban that whoever stole them should die and stood aside to let him search. When Laban reached Rachel's tent, she hid the teraphim by sitting on them and said she would not get up because she was menstruating. Jacob and laban then parted with a pact to preserve the peace between them.

In the morning, Jacob assembled his 4 wives and 11 sons, placing the maidservants and their children in front, Leah and her children next, and Rachel and Joseph in the rear. This could be that if Esau attacked them, Rachel and Joseph would be protected as they would be at the back.

Jacob moved home a further time while Rachel was Pregnant; near Bethlehem, Rachel went into labour and died as she gave birth to her second son Benjamin.

Jacob buried her and erected a monument over her grave. Rachel's Tomb, just outside Bethlehem.

Jacob loved Joseph more that his other children, Joseph even told his father all about his half-brothers Misdeeds.

His brothers became jealous of him.

When Joseph was seventeen, Jacob made a long coat of many colours for him. Seeing this, the half-brothers began to hate Joseph.

Then Joseph began to have dreams that implied that his family would bow down to him.

When he told his brothers about the dreams, it drove them to conspire against him. When Jacob heard of these dreams, he rebuked his son for proposing the idea that the house of Jacob would ever bow down to Joseph. Yet, he contemplated his son's words about these dreams (Genesis 37: 1-11).

Sometime afterward, the sons of Jacob by Leah, Bilhah and Zilpah, were feeding his flocks in Shechem. Jacob wanted to know how things were doing, so he asked Joseph to go down there and return with a report. This was the last time he would ever see his son in Hebron. Later that day, the report that Joseph had been killed came to Jacob, from Joseph's brothers who brought before him a coat laden with blood. Jacob identified the coat as the one he made for Joseph. At that moment he cried "it is my son's coat. A wild beast has killed him. Without doubt Joseph was torn to pieces". No one from the house of Jacob could comfort him.

The truth was that Joseph's brothers had attacked him and sold him into slavery on a caravan heading to Egypt.

Then they killed a goat and covered his coat with the blood.

Twenty years later, throughout the Middle East a severe famine occurred like none other that lasted seven years.

The word was that the only Kingdom still with corn was Egypt.

In the second year of the Famine, when Jacob was about 130 years old, he told his ten sons to go down to Egypt and buy some grain.

Benjamin stayed at home.

Nine of the sons returned to their fathers home from Egypt, Stockpiled with grain on their donkeys. They told their father what happened in Egypt.

They had been accused of being spies, their brother Simeon, had been taken prisoner. Then Reuben, the eldest, mentioned that they needed to bring Benjamin to Egypt to prove they are honest men, their father became furious with them. He couldn't understand how they were put in a position to tell the Egyptians all about their family. When the sons of Israel opened their sacks, they saw their money that they used to pay for the grain. It was still in their possession, and so they all became afraid. Israel then became angry with the loss of Joseph, Simeon, and now possibly Benjamin.

When the house of Israel had eaten all the grain that had been brought from Egypt, Israel told his sons to go back to Egypt and buy some more.

This time Judah spoke with his father, in order to try to persuade him to let Benjamin go with them.

Hoping to retrieve Simeon and get Benjamin back as well, Israel told them to take the best fruits of their land with them, and just in case there was a mistake when their money was returned with the grain, return this and offer double the amount to pay for more grain.

Israel then said "May God almighty give you mercy… if I am bereaved, I am bereaved!" (Genesis 43: 1-14).

When the sons of Israel returned the second time, they brought back with 20 extra donkeys carrying all kinds of goods and supplies as well as Egyptian transport Wagons.

When their father came out to meet them, his sons told him that Joseph was still alive, that he was the Governor over all of Egypt and that he wanted the house of Israel to move to Egypt.

Looking at the Wagons Israel then shouted "Joseph my son is alive. I will go and see him before I die" (Genesis 45: 16-28).

Israel and all of his house of seventy, gathered up all their belongings and their livestock and began the journey to Egypt.

On the way Israel stopped for the night at Beersheba to make a sacrificial offering to God.

When they arrive near the city where Joseph was, he sent Judah ahead to find out where the caravans should stop.

They were directed to disembark at Goshen.

It was there after 22 years, that Jacob met his son Joseph.

Eventually the time came for Joseph's family to meet the Pharaoh of Egypt.

The brothers came before the Pharaoh first, formally asking to stay on Egyptian lands.

The Pharaoh was honoured to meet Israel the father of his Governor Joseph. Thus Israel was able to bless the Pharaoh.

After the meeting, the families were directed to pasture in the land of Ramses where they lived in the province of Goshen.

The Final Days

Israel was 147 years old when he called for his favourite son Joseph and pleaded that he wasn't buried in Egypt.

He asked Joseph to have him carried to the land of Canaan to be buried with his forefathers.

Not long after Israel fell ill.

When Joseph came to visit him.

Israel declared that Ephraim and Manasseh would be the heirs of house of Israel.

Then Israel laid his right hand on the younger Ephraim's head and his left hand on the oldest Manasseh's head and blessed Joseph. However Joseph was not happy about this and so he switched his father's hands. But Israel refused saying, "but truly his younger brother shall be greater than he. " A declaration he made, just as Israel himself was himself to his firstborn brother Esau.

Then Israel called all his sons in and prophesied their blessings or curses to all twelve in order of their ages.

Afterwards, Israel died and the family, including the Egyptians, mourned him for seventy days. Israel was embalmed and a great ceremonial journey to Canaan was prepared by Joseph.

He led the servants of Pharaoh, and the elders of the houses Israel and Egypt beyond the Jordan River to Atad where they observed seven days of mourning.

Then they buried him in the cave of Machpelah, the property of Abraham when he bought it from the Hittites (Genesis 49: 33-50).

Let's look at Jacob.

His brother was very hungry after he had been out hunting.

He asked for some of the stew (and the venison in the pot was probable caught by Esau).

Instead of saying "help yourself brother" he demanded his brother's birth right.

Later with the support of his mother, he conned his father into receiving Esau birth right. (True Esau had already traded it with Jacob for the stew.

Again when we see people doing things like that, in our eyes it doesn't look Christian, but God rewards him and uses him.

Again there is still hope for us all.

Joseph

Joseph, son of Jacob and Rachel, lived in the land of Canaan with his ten half-brothers, one full brother, and a half-sister. Joseph was his father's favourite son, and this led to his brothers being jealous.

Jacob made a coat of many colours for Joseph, which angered his brothers even more.

When Joseph was seventeen years old, he had two dreams. In the first dream, Joseph and his brother gathered bundles of grain, of which those his brothers gathered bowed to his own.

In the second dream, the sun (father), the moon (mother), and eleven stars (brothers) bowed to Joseph himself. These dreams, implying his supremacy, angered his brothers even more   (Genesis 37: 1-11).

We know by reading about Jacob, the brothers eventually sold Joseph into slavery.

The Slavers on arriving in Egypt sold Joseph to Potiphar, the captain of Pharaoh's guard.

Later, Joseph became Potiphar's personal servant, and subsequently his household's superintendent. Here, Potiphar's wife Zuleika tried to seduce Joseph, which he refused. Angered by his running away from her, she made a false statement that Joseph had tried to rape her, and therefore he was put in prison (Genesis 39:1-20).

Joseph in prison

Joseph was a good prisoner, and so the head jailor put Joseph in charge of the other prisoners.

Later Pharaoh's chief cup bearer and the chief baker, who had upset the Pharaoh, were thrown into the prison, and had dreams which were interpreted by Joseph, who stated that the chief cup bearer would get his job back but the cook would be hanged. When the cup bearer was released from Prison, Joseph requested that he mentioned him to the Pharaoh and try to get him released from prison, but the cup bearer forgot about Joseph.

After two more years, the Pharaoh dreamt of seven withered ears of grain which devoured seven fat ears. When Pharaoh's advisors failed to interpret these dreams, the cup bearer remembered Joseph.

Joseph was summoned. He interpreted the dreams as seven years of abundance followed by seven years of famine, and advised the Pharaoh to store surplus grain.

Vizier of Egypt

Following the prediction, Joseph became Vizier or Governor, under the name of Zaphnath-Paaneah, and was given Asenath, the daughter of Potipherah, priest of On, to be his wife. During the seven years of abundance, Joseph ensured that the storehouses were full and that all produce was weighted. In the sixth year, Asenath had two children: Manasseh and Ephraim. When the famine came, it was so severe that people from surrounding nations came to Egypt to buy bread. The narrative also indicates that they went straight to Joseph or were directed to him, even by the Pharaoh himself.

(Genesis 41: 37-57). As a last resort, all of the inhabitants of Egypt, less the Priestly class, sold their properties to Joseph for seed; wherefore Joseph set a mandate that, because the people would be sowing and harvesting seed on government property, a fifth of the product should go to Pharaoh.

This mandate lasted until the days of Moses. (Genesis 47: 20-31).

Brothers sent to Egypt

Having read the previous pages about Jacob.

You would had read about Jacob sending ten of his sons to Egypt to buy grain.

When they had eaten all the grain, the brothers were sent back to Egypt a second time, to buy more grain.

This time they took Benjamin with them.

Joseph ordered his steward to load the brother's donkeys with food and all their money.

But Joseph also ordered that a silver cup be put in Benjamin's sack. The following morning the brothers began their journey home.

Joseph ordered his steward to go after the brothers and question them about the "missing" silver cup. When the Egyptians caught up with the brothers, they seized them and searched their sacks. This caused a stir among the brothers.

However they agreed to go back to Egypt. When the Vizier (Joseph) asked them about the silver cup, he demanded that the one who possessed the cup in his sack became his slave. In response, Judah pleaded with Joseph that Benjamin (whose sack the silver cup was found in) be allowed to return to his father, and he himself be kept as a slave. (Genesis 44).

The Vizier then broke down in tears, he could not control himself any longer and so he sent the Egyptian men out of the house. He then revealed to the Hebrews that he was their brother, Joseph.

The Brothers were frozen and were speechless. He brought them closer and told them what had happened and told them not to be afraid, that what they had meant for evil God had meant for Good. Then he commanded them to go and bring their father and their entire household down to Egypt and live in the province of Goshen, because there were five more years of famine left. So Joseph supplied them Egyptian transport wagons, new garments, money, and twenty extra donkeys carrying extra provisions for their journey (Genesis 45: 1-28).

Then Jacob (Israel) and his entire house of seventy, gathered up with all their livestock and travelled down to Egypt. Judah went ahead to ask Joseph where they should unload. They were directed to a province of Goshen.

It was here where Joseph met up with his father. It was twenty years since he last saw his father. There was much joy and rejoicing.

Jacob said "now let me die, since I have seen your face, because you are alive". (Genesis 46: 1-34)

The house of Israel had acquired many possessions and multiplied exceedingly during the course of seventeen years, even though the worst of the seven year famine. At this time, Jacob was 147 years old and bedridden. He had fallen ill and lost most of his vision. Israel asked Joseph that he not be buried in Egypt, he requested that he be carried to the land of Canaan to be buried with his forefathers,

Joseph buried his father in the cave of Machpellah, the property of Abraham.

Joseph lived to the age of 110, living to see his great-grandchildren. Before he died, he made the children of Israel swear that when they left Egypt they would take his bones with them, and he was embalmed and placed in a coffin in Egypt. (Genesis 50: 22-26).

The Children of Israel remembered their oath, and when they left Egypt during the Exodus, Moses took Joseph's bones with him. (Exodus 13: 19).

The Bones were buried at Shechem, in the parcel of ground which Jacob bought from the sons of Hamor (Joshua 24:32).

Joseph is described as a Minor prophet, true he doesn't have a large part, but this man behaved like I believe a Man of God should.

Always he worked hard and did his best, that's how he got promotion in The Captain of the Guards house.

He also fled from the Woman who tried to seduce him.

Then later we see him promoted to head at the prison.

When he met up with his brothers who had tried to kill him.

Did he kill them? No he told them "what they had meant for evil, God used for Good". He then forgave them.

1680 BC The book of Genesis comes to a close, having covered about 2300 years of history.

Ephraim

According to the book of Genesis, Ephraim was the second son of Joseph and Asenath. Arsenath was an Egyptian woman whom Pharaoh gave to Joseph as his wife, and the daughter of Potipherah, a priest of On. Ephraim was born in Egypt before the arrival of the children of Israel from Canaan.

The book of numbers lists three sons of Ephraim: Shuthelah, Beker, and Tahan. However, 1 Chronicles 7 claims that he had at least eight sons.

Jeroboam, the first King of the northern Kingdom of Israel, was also from the house of Ephraim.

Chapter Two - Moses to Samuel

Moses

The Israelites, settled in the land of Goshen in the time of Joseph and Jacob. Moses was born to his father Amram, son of Kehath the Levite, who entered Egypt with Jacob's household.

Moses was born in a time when his people, the Israelites, were an enslaved minority, they were increasing in numbers and the Egyptian Pharaoh was worried that they might ally themselves with Egypt's enemies. He decided to have all the new-born Hebrew boys killed in order to reduce the population of the Israelites.

The mother of "Moses", Jochebed, secretly hid him in a basket and covered it with bulrushes, then floated the basket on the River Nile.

The Pharaoh's daughter saw the basked and pulled it out of the river.

She saw the baby Moses.

The Baby was adopted and grew up with the Egyptian royal family.

The Princess needed a Woman to look after the baby, so Moses sister suggested Jochebed, So Moses mother brought her baby up.

Later when he was a man, he saw an Egyptian slave master beating a Hebrew slave. Moses was angry and killed the Egyptian.

Moses fled across the Red sea to Midian, where he saw a burning Bush on Mount Horeb (regarded as the mountain of God).

God told Moses to return to Egypt and demand the release of the Israelites from Egypt.

Moses argued that he was not a good speaker, so God allowed Aaron, his brother, to go with him and speak for him.

The Exodus

Moses went to the Pharaoh (who Moses new from his time with the royal family).

He did what God told him to do, he ordered the Pharaoh to release the Hebrew slaves and let them leave Egypt.

The Pharaoh was not impressed with this idea as he needed the slaves to do all the work in Egypt, so basically he told Moses in modern day language "on your Bike".

Moses then told the Pharaoh that if he did not let his people go, there would be ten plagues.

Again the Pharaoh refused and the ten plagues were released.

After the death of all the Egyptian first born male babies plague, which resulted in the death of the Pharaoh's youngest child.

Now the Pharaoh could see the power of the God of Moses and let the Hebrews go. Moses then led the people out of Egypt.

The Pharaoh later decided that he had made a mistake and sent his army after Moses in order to bring the Slaves back.

Moses was told about this and the shortest way to escape the Egyptians was to cross the Red sea.

God gave Moses the power to divide the Red sea so the Hebrews could escape.

When the pursuing Egyptians were half way across, the Waters closed, and most of the Egyptian army was killed.

The Israelites headed to Mount Sinai where they camped for a while.

While camped here, Moses went up the mountain and God gave him two tablets with the Ten Commandments on.

These were the Laws of God.

Moses was a long time up the mountain, some of the people feared that he might be dead, so they made a statue of a golden calf and began to worship it, thus disobeying and angering both God and Moses. Moses, out of anger, broke the tablets, and later ordered the elimination of those who worshiped the golden statue, which was melted down and fed to the idolaters. (Now that sounds painful).

He also wrote the Ten Commandments on a new set of tablets.

Moses delivered the laws of God to the Israelites, instituted the Priesthood under the sons of Moses' brother Aaron.

God gave Moses instructions for the Tabernacle, the mobile shrine by which he would travel with the Israelites to the Promised Land.

The Hebrews wandered through the desert for 40 years.

The Israelites had a tendency to whine and complain about everything, including their leaders.

Sometime after leaving Egypt they had a dire need for water, instead of asking and having faith in God, they turned to complaining against their human leaders who were Moses and Aaron. They whined about being brought out to the wilderness so that, they assumed, both they and all they possessed would be no more.

"Why did you bring us out of Egypt into this miserable place where nothing will grow? There is not even any water to drink" (Numbers 20:5).

God told Moses and Aaron that they were to, before all the people that left Egypt, strike a certain rock with Aaron's staff, after they did this, water came from the rock to quell the thirst of the people.

The two men did what God commanded, except that they were so angry with the people that they made it appear as if they by their own power were providing water " hear now, you rebels! Must we bring more water for you out of this rock?" (Numbers 20:10).

Moses then struck the rock again.

God leaves no doubt as to why his two chosen leaders didn't go into the land of milk and honey promised to Abraham, and Jacob.

The Lord spoke to Moses and Aaron, "because you did not believe me, to hallow in the eyes of the children of Israel, therefore you shall not bring this assembly into the land that I have given them". (Numbers 20:12).

Moses died within sight of the Promised Land, he had climbed up Mount Nebo to the top of Pisgah.

Joshua led the Israelites into the Promised Land after the death of Moses. (1451 BC).

Moses is regarded as the writer of the first five books in the Bible.

Which together comprise the Torah, the first and most revered section of the Hebrew Bible.

The New Testament states that after the death of Moses, Michael the Archangel and the devil disputed over his body (Jude 1:9)

Well what a man. He was saved from death as a baby.

Brought up in the Royal palace.

Then he brought the Israelites out of Egypt.

In the power of God he did many miracles.

He became the lawmaker of the Hebrews, and wrote the Torah.

But he often showed anger (like we all do).

Killed an Egyptian slave master.

He lost the plot when the people kept moaning about no water.

Defiantly a man of God but he still had the problems we have. So still hope for us

When Moses found the people worshiping the golden calf, he smashed the tablets with the Ten Commandments on.

He then went back up the mountain and told God he was fed up with the people, only to find God felt the same.

This was a key moment in Israel's history.

God told Moses that he was about to blot Israel out of his book. Moses then said that he also should be blotted out as he did not want to be left alone. He effectively was saying "take my life as an atonement".

God explained that he only blots out of his book the names of those who have sinned against him, Moses insisted that the people were punished, and God told him to deal with the ringleaders.

Christians

The Book of Exodus can be applied to Christians.

Paul reflecting on some of the events in Exodus, writes to the Church of Corinth, "These things occurred as examples, to keep us from setting our hearts on evil things, as they did."

We need to always make sure our Name is in Gods book.

God showed many times in this story how much he loved the Israelites, but they often returned to sinning against him.

They were punished but whenever they repented, God forgave them and loved them even more.

Aaron

The only evidence about Aaron and Moses comes from religious texts such as the Bible and the Quran.

Aaron was the older brother of Moses. Aaron and his elder sister Miriam remained with the family in the Eastern border-land of Egypt (Goshen).

Moses had problems speaking to people in authority so Aaron became his brother's spokesman.

Aaron became the first High Priest of the Israelites

At the command of Moses his Rod turned into a large snake.

Then he stretched out his staff in order to start the first three plagues. After this Moses was able to Speak and act for himself.

At the battle of Amalek; he was chosen with Hur to support the hand of Moses that held the "rod of God" (Exodus 17:9).

The Books of Exodus, Leviticus, and Numbers maintain that Aaron received from God a monopoly over the Priesthood for himself and male descendants (Exodus 28:1), the family of Aaron had the exclusive right and responsibility to make offerings on the Alter to the God of Israel.

The Priests were also commissioned to bless the people (Numbers 6: 22-27).

What is clear is that High Priests claiming Aaronide descent dominated the second Temple period.

Aaron plays a leading role in several stories of conflicts over leadership during Israel's wilderness wanderings. During the long instance of Moses on Mount Sinai, the people provoked Aaron to make a Golden Calf as a visible image of the divinity who had delivered them from Egypt (Exodus 32: 1-6).

This incident almost caused God to destroy the Israelites for their unfaithfulness to the Covenant (Exodus 32:10). Moses successfully intervened, but then led the loyal Levites in executing the culprits and a plague afflicted those who were left (Exodus 32:25-35).

Aaron was a lucky boy here because of the intercession of Moses according to Deuteronomy 9:20.

The Pentateuch generally depicts Moses, Aaron and Miriam, as the leaders of Israel after the Exodus, this is shown in the book of Micah.

Aaron, like Moses, were not permitted to enter Canaan with the Israelites. This you can read about in the Moses section.

There are two accounts of the death of Aaron in the Pentateuch. Numbers says that soon after the incident at Meribah, Aaron with his son Eleazar and Moses ascended Mount Hor, There Moses stripped Aaron of his Priestly garments and transferred them to Eleazar. Aaron died on the summit of the mountain, and people mourned for him thirty days (Numbers 20:22-29).

The second account is found in Deuteronomy 10:6, where Aaron died at Moserah and was buried.

There is a significant amount of distance between these two points, as the itinerary in Numbers 33:31-37 records seven stages between Moseroth and Mount Hor.

Chosen be God to be a prophet and the first High Priest of the Israelites. And yet he under pressure and maybe fear of death, let the people build the Golden calf.

If people were threatening to kill you, if you refused to build this idol, would you build it? Only we can answer this if we were in the same situation.

Miriam

Miriam was the elder sister of Moses by seven years, and four years older that Aaron.

She was a Prophet and first appears in the book of Exodus.

In Exodus 2, it reads that her mother Yocheved's request, Miriam hid her baby brother Moses by the side of a river to avoid Pharaoh's soldiers finding him and killing him, under his order to kill all the new-born Hebrew babies.

Miriam watched as the Pharaoh's daughter found the baby and decided to adopt him. Miriam then suggested to her, that it may be good if Yocheved would be a good nurse for the baby. As a result, Moses was raised to be familiar with his background as a Hebrew.

Miriam danced and sang a victory song recorded briefly in the Bible as the shorter "song of the sea" after Pharaoh's army was drowned in the Red sea (Exodus 15:20-21).

Numbers 12 states that Aaron and Miriam both objected to the marriage of Moses to a Cushite woman, to which God responds by appearing in a Pillar of cloud and showing support for Moses. Afterwards, only Miriam is struck with Izaraal, (Leprosy) after Aaron asks Moses to intercede for her, Moses asks God to heal her and she recovers within seven days. (Numbers 12).

A passage in Micah states: "And I brought you forth out of the Land of Egypt, and redeemed you from the house of bondage, and I sent before you Moses, Aaron and Miriam." (Micah 6:4)

Marriage

Miriam was the Wife of Hur who is mentioned in Exodus as a companion of Moses.

Death

When the Israelites on their journey to the land of Canaan came into the wilderness of Zin in the first month, and the people stayed in Kadesh, Miriam died and was buried there.

After her death, a spring of abundant water called Meribah opened.   (Numbers 20:7-13).

In Leviticus, no new prophets are mentioned. In Numbers we read about two Minor Prophets, Eldad and Medad.

Seventy Elders had left the camp and had gone to the Tabernacle to receive the ability to prophesy from God.

While they were away, Eldad and Medad prophesied among the Israelites.

Joshua asked Moses to forbid Eldad and Medad from prophecy, but Moses argued that it was a good thing that others could prophesy, and that ideally all the Israelites would prophesy.

Eldad and Medad predicted a war with Gog and Magog, with the king from Magog uniting the Non-Jews and launching war in Palestine against the Jews, but these non-Jews were defeated and slain by fire from the Throne of God.

According to biblical scholars, the real purpose of the story was to indicate that prophecy was not restricted to a few people.

There are no new Prophets mentioned in Deuteronomy.

Here ends the first five books of the Bible attributed to be written by Moses.

And also known as the Torah by the Hebrews.

Joshua

His name was Hoshe'a, the son of Nun, of the tribe of Ephraim, but Moses called him Yehoshu'a.

After the death of Moses he became the leader of the Israelites.

The Israelites entered the Promised Land in 1425 (Geneses 12).

Joshua was a major figure in the book of Exodus. He was given the job by Moses of selecting and commanding an army for their first battle after leaving Egypt, against the Amalekites in Rephidim (Exodus 17:8-16), in which they were victorious.

Later he went with Moses when he climbed Mount Sinai to talk with God, visualize God's plan for the Israelite Tabernacle and receive the Ten Commandments.

When they descended the Mountain and heard the Israelites celebrating around the golden calf, Moses broke the tablets bearing the words of the commandments.

When Moses climbed back up the mountain, to re-create the tablets recording the Ten Commandments, Joshua was not with him.

Joshua was one of the twelve spies that were sent into the land of Canaan. (Numbers 13:16-17), but only he and Caleb gave an encouraging report. A reward for which would be that only these two of their entire generation would enter the Promised Land (Numbers 14:22-24).

Conquest of Canaan

At the Jordan River, the waters parted, as they had for Moses at the Red Sea. The first battle after the crossing of the Jordan was the Battle of Jericho. Joshua led the destruction of Jericho, then moved onto Ai, a small neighbouring city to the west. However they were defeated with thirty six Israelite deaths. The defeat was down to Achan taking an "accursed thing" from Jericho; which was followed by Achan and his family and his animals being stoned to death to restore Gods favour. Joshua then went on to defeat Ai.

The Israelites faced an alliance of Amorite Kings from Jerusalem, Hebron, Jarmuth, Lachish, and Eglon. At Gibeon

Joshua asked God to cause the sun and moon to stand still, so that he could finish the battle in day light

"The Lord heeded the voice of a man, for the Lord fought for Israel" (Joshua 10:14). He also hurled huge hailstones from the sky which killed more Canaanites than those which the Israelites killed.

Joshua led the Israelites to several victories, taking much of Canaan.

He presided over the Israelite gatherings at Gilgal and Shiloh which allowed land to be allocated to the tribes of Israel (Joshua 14: 1-5) and the Israelites rewarded him with the Ephraimite city of Timaath-Semnath, where he settled.

Death

When Joshua was very old, Joshua gathered the elders and chiefs of the Israelites and begged them not to have any fellowship with the native population, because it could lead to them being unfaithful to God, he took leave of the people, telling them to be loyal to God.

At a general assembly of the clans at Shechem. He took leave of his people, admonished them to be loyal to God. Joshua then set up a great stone under an oak by the sanctuary of God.

Soon afterwards he died, he was 110, the same age as Joseph when he died.

He was buried at Timnath-heres, in the hill country of Ephaim, north of Gaash.

The book of Joshua, is not a well-known book. The Author believed to be Joshua himself, selects the events which are most significant to God, or are explained by God's activity. The real hero of this book is not Joshua but God.

About two and a half million slaves, men, women and children. From babies to old people. They had no military training at all. They entered the Promised Land, a land full of well-fortified cities. Only with the Power of God could they conquer this Land.

Joshua was 80 years old when he was asked to be the leader of the Israelites after the death of Moses.

Joshua sent two spies into Jericho, mirroring the two spies which returned from the Promised Land with good news.

When the Israelites entered the Promised Land, God stopped sending Manna. Jericho was the first city to be attacked.

The night before the battle, Joshua approached the city under darkness to check out the fortifications.

On the way he was met by a man.

Joshua asked this man if he was friend or foe. He was very surprised to hear a reply of "no" a nonsensical reply.

The man replied that he was neither a Jew nor a Canaanite, but part of God's forces. He was in fact none other than a captain of the Lords hosts, an Archangel.

Joshua was being reminded that he was only a under officer. It also made clear that he did not fight alone.

Wasn't this wonderful? Joshua and his army of untrained men were about to attack Jericho a well-built city.

He must had been thinking "how are we going to do this", then an Archangel turned up and said don't worry, God is in charge and we angels are also here to help you. That must had been some relief for Joshua.

Also Joshua was shown that he was not the true commander of Israel.

The last verses of the book record three burials: the burial of Joshua, the burial of Joseph's bones and the burial of Eleazer.

For forty years they had carried with them a coffin containing Joseph's bones, because his dying wish was to be buried in the Promised Land.

The book of Joshua is best summed up in two phases:

Without God they could not had done it.

Without them God would not had done it.

One final section

One of the most amazing things that God has for us today happened recently to the astronauts and space scientists at green belt, Indiana. They were checking the position of the sun, moon and planets out in space where they would be in 100 years and 1,000 years from now.

They have to know this in order that they do not send up a satellite and have it collide with something later on, on one of its orbits. They have to lay out the orbit in terms of the life of the satellite and where the planets will be so that the whole thing will not go wrong.

They ran the computer measurements backwards and forwards over the centuries and it came to a halt. The computer stopped and put up a red signal which meant that there was something wrong either with the information fed into it or with the results as compared with the standards. They called in the service department to check it out and they said," it's perfect." The head of the operation said, "What's wrong"?

Well. We've found there's a day missing in space in a lapsed time. They were puzzled and there seemed no answer. Then one man on the team remembered he'd been told at Sunday school of the sun standing still. They didn't believe him but as no alternative was coming they asked him to get a Bible and find it.

This he did Book of Joshua 10:12-14, and the sun stood still, and the moon stayed, and did not go down the whole day.

The space scientist said "there is the missing day".

Amen

1400 The Beginning of Judges and their governing of Israel, covered about 305 years (ca 1095BC,) see 1 Samuel 8.

Deborah

Deborah, was a prophet of God, the fourth Judge of pre-Monarchy Israel, counsellor, warrior, and wife of Lapidoth according to the book of Judges Chapters 4 and 5. The only female judge mentioned in the Bible. Deborah (being a prophetess) told Barak that the Lord God of Israel commanded him to lead an attack against the army of Jabin King of Canaan and his military commander Sisera (Judges 4: 6-7); the entire story is recounted in chapter 4.

Song of Deborah

Here in chapter 5, we have the same story in Poetic form.

This song could date from 12th century BC, and is perhaps the earliest sample of Hebrew poetry.

In Hebrew her name means Busy Bee.

She delivered her judgements beneath a date palm tree between Ramah in Benjamin and Bethel in the land of Ephraim. (Judges 4:5)'

The people of Israel had been oppressed by Jabin, the King of Canaan, who's Capital was Hazor, for twenty years. Stirred by the wretched condition of Israel she sends to Barak, the son of Abinoam, at Kedesh of Naphali, and tells him that the Lord God had commanded him to gather ten thousand troops of Naphtali and Zebulun and concentrate them upon Mount Tabor, the mountain at the northern angle of the great Plain of Esdraelon. At the same time she states that the Lord God of Israel will draw Sisera to the river Kishon. Barak declines to go without the prophet. Deborah consents to go, but declares that the glory of the Victory will therefore belong to a woman. As soon as the news of the rebellion reaches Sisera he collects nine hundred chariots of iron and a host of people.

Then Deborah said, according to Judges 4:14. Go! This is the day the Lord has given Sisera into your hands. Has not the Lord gone ahead of you? So Barak went down Mount Tabor, with ten thousand men following him.

As Deborah prophesied, a battle is fought (led by Barak), and Sisera is completely defeated. He himself escaped on foot, while his army is pursued as far as Harosheth of the Gentiles and destroyed.

Sisera comes to the tent of Jael; and he lies down to rest. He asked for a drink; Jael gives him milk; and while he is asleep she hammers a tent peg through his temple.

The Biblical account of Deborah ends with the statement that after the battle, there was peace in the land for 40 years. (Judges 5: 31).

Deborah Judged the Israelites for 40 years (Judges 5.31).

From 1107 until her death in 1067 BC.

Gideon

Gideon was one of the most feared men in the bible.

He was a Military leader, Judge and Prophet whose calling and victory over the Midianites is recorded in the Bible in chapters 6-8.

Gideon was the son of Joash, from the Abiezrite clan in the tribe of Manasseh and lived in Ephra (Ophrah). As a leader of the Israelites, he won a decisive victory over a Midianite army despite a vast numbers disadvantage, leading a troop of 300 brave men.

As is the pattern throughout the book of Judges, the Israelites again turned away from God after 40 years of peace brought by Deborah's victory over Canaan, and Midianites, Amalekites and other Bedouin people harry Israel for seven years. God chose Gideon, a young man from the tribe of Manasseh, to free the people of Israel and to condemn their idolatry. The Angel of the Lord. Came as a traveller who sat down in the shade (of the Terebinth tree) to enjoy a little refreshment and repose, and entered into conversation with Gideon.

This is similar to the meeting between Abraham and the visitors who came to him in the terebinith trees of Mamre and promised Abraham and Sarah, in their old age, that they would have a son.

The Angel of the Lord greeted Gideon:

The Lord is with you, you mighty man of valour.

Gideon asked for proof of God's will by three miracles: the first was a sign from the angel of the Lord, in which the angel appeared to Gideon and caused fire to shoot up out of a rock (Judges 6: 11-22), and then two signs involving a fleece, performed on consecutive nights and the exact opposite of each other (Judges 6: 36-40).

On God's instructions, Gideon destroyed the town's altar to Baal and the symbol of the goddess Asherah beside it, receiving the byname of Jerubbaal from his father:

He sent out messengers to gather together men from the tribes of Asher, Zebulun, and Naphtali, as well as his own tribe of Manasseh, in order to meet an armed force of the people of Midian and the Amalek that had crossed the Jordan River, and they were camped at the well of Harod in the valley of Jezreel. But God informed Gideon that the men he had gathered were too many, with so many men, there would be reason for the Israelites to claim the victory as their own instead of acknowledging that God had saved them. God first instructed Gideon to send home those who were afraid. Gideon invited any man who wanted to leave, to do so; 22,000 men returned home and 10,000 remained. Yet with that number, God told Gideon they were still too many and instructed him to bring them to the water and to keep only those who raised the water to their mouth, and while doing so, drank the water lapping it with their tongues as a dog laps. This amounted to 300 men (Judges 7: 4-7).

During the night, God instructed Gideon to approach the Midianite camp. There, Gideon overheard a Midianite man tell a friend of a dream in which" a loaf of barley bread tumbled into the camp of Midian", causing their tents in the camp to collapse. This was interpreted as meaning that God had given the Midianites over to Gideon. Gideon returned to the Israelite camp and gave each of his men a trumpet (Shofar) and a clay jar with a torch hidden inside. Divided into three companies, Gideon and the three hundred marched on the enemy camp. He instructed them to blow the trumpet, give a battle cry and light torches, simulating an attack by a large force. As they did so, the Midianite army fled (Judges 7: 17-22).

Gideon sent messengers ahead into Israel calling for the Ephraimites to pursue the retreating Midiamites and two of their leaders, Oreb and Zeeb. Gideon and the three hundred pursued Zebah and Zalmunna, the two Midianite kings. When he asked for provisions in his pursuit, the men of Succoth and Peniel refused and taunted Gideon. After capturing the two kings, Gideon punished the men of Succoth, and pulled down the tower of Peniel killing all the men there. Gideon invited his eldest son, Jether, to kill Zebah and Zalmunna, but being young at the time, did not have the confidence to carry out his father's request, so Zebah and Zalmunna called on Gideon to kill them. Gideon then killed them both as justice for the death of his brothers (Judges 8: 19-21).

The Israelites asked Gideon to be their King, but he refused, telling them that only God was their ruler (Judges 8: 22-23).

Gideon went on to make an Ephod out of the gold won in the battle, which eventually caused the whole of Israel again to turn away from God yet again. Gideon had 70 sons from many women he took as wives. He also had a Shechemite concubine who bore him a son names (Abimelech).

There was peace in Israel for another 40 years during the life of Gideon. As soon as Gideon died of old age, the Israelites again turned to worship the false god Baal-Berith and ignored the family of Gideon (Judges 8: 33).

In the New Testament, Gideon is mentioned in Chapter 11 of Hebrews as an example of a man of faith.

Following the Death of Gideon. His son Abimelech asked the people if they would prefer his leadership to the leadership of his 70 brothers as a group. The people chose him.

He then proceeds to murder his other brothers (Judges 9:4).

Only the youngest brother Jotham escaped.

Things got steadily worst in his hunger for power, with little interest in the welfare of his people.

Eventually he was killed in battle.

The book of Ruth was written at the same time as Judges but could hardly be a greater contrast between the two.

When a Judge died, there was a gap before another one was appointed.

Each time the people reverted to the type of behaviour which led to God's punishment.

Let's stop a while here.

As the Israelites keep going back to worshiping Baal and other idols, and the things which go with this.

Why doesn't God just destroy them?

I think that if I was God I may get really fed up with them.

Lucky I am not God.

If I look at myself. How many times have I done wrong, repented, asked for forgiveness, and then done wrong again.

I give thanks that God, is a God of love.

Who is patient and kind and a forgiving God?

He loves me and you and is willing to forgive again and again.

What a loving Father we have.

Samuel

There are no new Prophets in the book of Ruth.

Samuel's Mother was Hannah and his Father was Elkanah.

Elkanah lived at Pama-thaim in the district of Zuph.

According to genealogical tables, Elkanah was a Levite.

Elkanah had two wives, Peninnah and Hannah. Peninnah had children, Hannah did not.

Hannah was the favourite of Elkanah, this made Peninnah jealous, and she put Hannah down for her lack of children.

Elkanah and Hannah were devout followers of God.

Hannah once went to a sanctuary and prayed for a child. In tears, she vowed that were she granted a child, she would dedicate him to God as a Nazirine.

Eli who was sitting at the foot of the doorpost in the sanctuary at Shiloh, saw her mumbling to herself and thought she was drunk, but is soon assured of her motivation and that she was not drunk.

Eli was the Priest of Shiloh, and one of the last Israelite Judges before the rule of Kings in ancient Israel. He had taken leadership after Samson's death. Eli blessed her and she went home. Later, Hannah became pregnant, her child was Samuel.

Hannah's song of thanksgiving resembles in parts Mary's later Magnificat.

After the child was weaned, she left him in Eli's care and only visited from time to time.

Calling

One night, Samuel heard a voice calling his name. Samuel was about 12 years old. He thought it was coming from Eli and went to Eli to ask what he wanted, Eli sent Samuel back to his bed.

After this had happened three times, Eli realized that the voice was from God, and told Samuel how to answer. Once Samuel responded, the Lord told him that the wickedness of the sons of Eli had resulted in their dynasty being destroyed.

In the morning, Eli asked Samuel to tell him what happened and told to him by God. Upon hearing what God had said, he said that God should do what he felt was right.

Leader

During Samuels's youth at Shiloh, the Philistines inflected a decisive defeat against the Israelites at Eben-Ezer, placed the land under the control of the Philistines, and took the sanctuary's Arc for themselves. Upon hearing the bad news of the capture of the Arc of the Covenant, and the death of his sons, Eli collapsed and died.

When the Philistines had been in possession of the Arc of the Covenant for about 7 months and had been visited with calamities and misfortunes, they decided to return the Arc to the Israelites.

After 20 years of oppression, Samuel, had gained prominence as a Prophet (1 Samuel 3:20), summoned the people to the hill of Mizpah, and led them against the Philistines. The Philistines, having marched to Mizpah to attack the new Israelite army, were well beaten and fled in terror. The retreating Philistines were slaughtered by the Israelites. Then Samuel built a large statue at the site of the battle, after there was a long period of peace,

King Maker

Originally Samuel had appointed two of his sons as successors, just like Eli's sons, Samuels proved unworthy. The Israelites rejected them, because of the external threat from other tribes, such as the Philistines, the tribal leaders decided that there was a need for a more unified, central government, and demanded Samuel appoint a King.

Samuel saw this as a personal rejection, and at first was reluctant to carry out their wishes. Later he was reassured by a divine revelation. He warns the people of the potential negative consequences of such a decision. Samuel was a known Chozeh, a seer believed to be endowed with the true spiritual insight, in contrast to the false prophets, of the neighbouring nations. When Saul and his servant were searching for his father's lost asses, the servant suggested consulting the nearby Samuel. Samuel recognized Saul as the future King.

Just before his retirement, Samuel gathered the people together at Gilgal, and gave them a farewell speech in which he emphasised how Prophets and judges were more important than Kings, how Kings should be held to account, and how people should never fall into idol worship, or worship of asherah or of baal; Samuel threatened that God would subject the people to foreign invaders if they disobey.

This is seen by some as a deuteronomic redaction, since archaeological finds indicate the asherah was still worshiped in Israelite homes well into the 6th century BC.

However the Bible says in 1 Kings 11: 5, 33, and 2 Kings 23: 13 that the Israelites fell into asherah worship later on.

When Saul was preparing to fight the philistines, Samuel denounces him for proceeding with the pre-battle sacrifice without waiting for the overdue Samuel to arrive. He prophesies that Saul's rule will see no dynastic succession.

During the campaign against the Amalekites, King Saul spared Agag, the king of the Amalekites, and the best of their livestock. Saul tells Samuel that he spared the choicest of the Amalekites' sheep and oxen, intending to sacrifice the livestock to God. This was a violation of the Lord's command, as pronounced by Samuel, to " utterly destroy all that they have , and spare nothing; slay men and women, infant and suckling, ox and sheep, camel and ass" (1 Samuel 15:3).

Samuel confronts Saul for his disobedience and tells him that God made him King, and God can replace him as King. Samuel then proceeded to execute Agag, Saul never saw Samuel alive again after this.

Samuel went to Bethlehem and secretly anoints David as King. He would later provide sanctuary for David, when Saul first tried to have David Killed.

Samuel died and was buried in Ramah. Aged 52.

Saul later had the witch of Endor conjure Samuels's ghost in order to predict the result of an up-coming battle. Samuel was terrified by the ordeal, having expected to be appearing to face God's judgement, and had therefore brought Moses with him (to the land of the living) as a witness to this adherence to mityvot.

Samuel clearly is a man of God.

Chapter Three - Saul to Iddo

Saul

Saul is classified as a minor prophet, although not on the list of twelve Minor Prophets.

Saul was anointed by the prophet Samuel and he reigned from Gibeah.

He was the first King of the United Kingdom of Israel and Judah.

He eventually fell on his sword (committed suicide) to avoid capture in the battle against the Philistines at Mount Gilboa, during which three of his sons were also killed.

According to the Tanakh, Saul was the son of Kish, of the family of the Matrites, and a member of the tribe of Benjamin, one of the twelve tribes of Israel. It appears that he came from Gilbeah.

Saul married Ahinoam, daughter of Ahimaaz. They had four sons and two daughters. The sons were Jonathan, Abinadab, Malchishua and Ish-bosheth. Their daughters were named Merab and Michal.

Saul also had a concubine named Rizpah, daughter of Aiah, who bore him two sons, Armoni and Mephibosheth. (2 Samuel 21: 8).

Saul died at the Battle of Mount Gilboa (1 Samuel 31:3-6), and was buried in Zelah, in the region of Benjamin (2 Samuel 21:14).

Three of Saul's sons Jonathan, and Abinadab, and Malchishua died with him at Mount Gilboa (1 Samuel 31:2).

Ish-Bosheth became king of Israel, at the age of forty. At David's request Abner had Michal returned to David. Ish-bosheth reigned for two years, but after the death of Abner, was killed by two of his own captains. Armoni and Mephibosheth (Saul's sons by the Concubine, Rizpah) were given by David along with the five sons of Merab (Saul's daughter) to the Gibeonites, who claimed them. (2 Samuel 21:8-9)

The only Male descendant of Saul was Mephibosheth, Jonathan's lame son, who was 5 when his father and grandfather were killed. In time, he came under the protection of David.

Saul among the Prophets

Having been anointed by Samuel, Saul is told of signs indicating that he has been divinely appointed. The last of these is that Saul will be met by an ecstatic group of prophets leaving a high place and playing the lyre, tambourine, and flutes. Saul encounters the ecstatic prophets and joins them. Later, Saul sends men to pursue David, but when they meet a group of ecstatic prophets playing music, they become possessed by a prophetic state and join in. Saul sends more men, but they too join the prophets. Eventually Saul himself goes, and also joins the prophets. (1 Samuel 19: 24).

Saul and David

After Samuel had told Saul that God had rejected him as king, David, a son of Jesse, from the tribe of Judah, enters the story: from this point on Saul's story is largely the account of his troubled relationship with David.

Saul is troubled by an evil spirit sent by God. He requests soothing music, and a servant recommends David the son of Jesse, who is renowned as a skilful harpist and soldier. When word of Saul's needs reach Jesse, he sends David, who had been looking after a flock, and David is appointed as Saul's armour bearer and remains at court playing the harp as needed to calm Saul during his troubled spells.

The Philistines return with an army to attack Israel, and the Philistines and Israelites forces gather on opposite sides of a valley. The Philistine's champion Goliath issues a challenge for single combat, but none of the Israelite accept. David a young shepherd boy happens to be delivering food to his three elder brothers in the army, and he hears Goliath's challenge. David speaks mockingly of the Philistines to some soldiers; his speech is overheard and reported to Saul, who calls for David and appoints him as his champion. David easily defeats Goliath with a single shot from a sling.

Saul fear's David's growing popularity and views him as a rival to the throne.

Saul's son Jonathan and David become best friends. Jonathan recognizes David as the rightful King.

On two occasions Saul threw a spear at David as he played the harp for Saul. Now Saul is actively plotting against David.

Saul sends assassins in the night to kill David, but Michal helps him escape.

As this section is about the Minor prophet Saul and not David I will move onto Nathan and Gad two other prophets in Samuel.

I know that Saul is only classified as a minor prophet, but clearly Saul has some spiritual problems. But then don't we all.

The Kings Prophets of the old Testament

Nathan, Gad and Shemaiah, have little written about them. But they are clearly prophets.

Nathan

According to 2 Samuel, he was a court prophet who lived in the time of King David. He Announced to David the Covenant God was making with him(2 Samuel 7.) and he came to David to reprimand him over his committing adultery with Bathsheba while she was the wife of Uriah the Hittite whose death had also arranged to hid his previous transgression (2 Samuel 11-12).

It is Nathan who tells the dying David of the plot of Adonijah to become King, resulting in Solomon being proclaimed King instead.

Gad

Gad was a seer or Prophet in the Bible. He was one of the personal prophets of King David of Israel and some of his writings are believed to be included in the Books of Samuel.

After David confesses his sin of taking a census of the people of Israel and Judah, God sends Gad to David to offer him his choice of three forms of punishment.

Gad goes to David and tells him to build an altar to God after he stops the plague that David chose as punishment.

Shemaiah

Shemaiah was a prophet in the reign of Rehoboam (1 Kings 12:22-24). He is venerated as a saint in the liturgical calendar of the Eastern Orthodox Church on January 8.

He is best known for two advents:

> 1 / Preventing Rehoboam from war with Jeroboam- 1 Kings 12: 22-24; 2 Chronicles 11: 2-4;

2/ Prophesying the punishment of Rehoboam by Shisak, King of Egypt- 2 Chronicles 12: 5, 7.

King Rehoboam had assembled 180, 000 troops to forcefully bring back the ten rebellious tribes.

Shemaiah was a "man of God", and prophesies in verse 24 that this thing is from the Lord, and they are not to go up against the Northern Tribes, so "everyone returned to their own homes".

Iddo

Iddo or Eido – 1 Kings 4:14 was a minor Prophet, again not one of the list of twelve, who lived during the reigns of King Solomon and his heirs, Rehoboam and Abijah, in the Kingdom of Judah.

Little is known about Iddo but he appears in the books of Chronicles, Iddo seems to have been quite prolific in his time, with his Prophecies concerning the rival King Jeroboam 1 of Israel recorded in the lost book of visions (2 Chronicles 9: 29).

He also wrote a history of King Rehoboam , known as the "words of Shemaiah the prophet and Iddo the seer" (2 Chronicles 12:15).

Rashi, identifies him with the unidentified "man of God" from 1 Kings 13: 1. Iddo , on account of his prophecies against Jeroboam, has been identified by Josephus and Jerome with the prophet who denounced the altar of

Jeroboam and who was afterwards killed by a lion for having disobeyed the Lord's command to not eat or drink on the way back from having prophesized to Jeroboam. His remains were laid to rest in the tomb of a prophet of Samaria who had detained him.

300 years later during the reign of King Josiah when Jeroboam's altar was defiled by burning human bones on them by order of King Josiah, the King asked whose tombstone this was; he was told it was that of the "man of God" who predicted the doom of the altar and of the Bethel prophet, Josiah ordered the tomb to be left in peace as this prophecy had been fulfilled (2 Kings 16-18).

Another Iddo is mentioned in Ezra 8:17 as the chief man at the place Casiphia. Ezra requests assistance from Iddo and his brethren to bring servants for the Temple. It is this Iddo Ezra refers to when he calls the prophet Zechariah a "son of Iddo" in Ezra 5:1 and 6:14. The book of Zechariah 1:1 and 1:7 mention Iddo as the paternal grandfather of Zechariah.

Biblical Timeline

975 After Solomon's death, Rehoboam succeeds Solomon as King (1 Kings 12, some have 931 as the date)). The Kingdom is divided.

When Solomon died, the fight for his throne results in the twelve tribes of Israel dividing, creating the Great Schism. The two southern tribes, Benjamin and Judah, maintaining Jerusalem as their capital, become "The Kingdom of Judah" under the reign of Rehoboam. He reigns 17 years. The Ten Northern tribes of Israel revolt becoming "The Kingdom of Israel" under the leadership of Jeroboam. He reigns 21 years. Israel's continued, with 19 Kings from the reign of Solomon, for 254 years. Israel makes Samaria its Capital.

721 The Assyrians capture Samaria and take Israel captive (CP 2 Chronicles 33, end of the Kingdom of Israel).

597 Jerusalem is captured by Babylon (2 Chronicles.36)

536 First group returns from captivity (see Ezra 8).

458 The Second group returns from bondage (Ezra 8).

444 The walls of Jerusalem are rebuilt under the leadership of Nehemiah (Nehe. 1-7).

398 The Completion of the 39 books that constitute the "Old Testament" see Malachi). This date began the "400 years of Silence" between the book of Malachi and the book of Matthew (New Testament).

Chapter Four - Prophets of Israel: Alijah to Oded

Alijah

Alijah the Shilonite, was a Levite prophet of Shiloh in the days of Solomon.

Alijah encouraged a revolt against Solomon and foretold to Jeroboam that he would become King (1 Kings 11:29).

In 1 Kings 11: 31-39, he announced the separation of the Northern ten tribes from Solomon's united Kingdom, forming the Northern Kingdom. In 1 Kings 14:6-16, Alijah's prophesy, delivered to Jeroboam's wife, foretold the death of the King's son, the destruction of Jeroboam's dynasty, and the fall and captivity of Israel " beyond the river", (the land East of the Euphrates).

Micaiah

Micaiah, son of Imiah, is a prophet. He is not to be confused with Micah, prophet of the book of Micah.

The events leading up to the appearance of Micaiah are in 1 Kings 22:1-12. In 1 Kings 22:1-4, Jehoshaphat, the king of Judah goes to visit the King of Israel (identified in 1 Kings 22:20 as Ahab), and asked if he could go with him to take Ramoth-gilead which was under the rule of the King of Aram.

Jehoshaphat the Judahite requests that Ahab the Israelite, "first inquire of the word of the Lord" (1 Kings 22: 5). Ahab then calls on his prophets and asks if he should go into battle against Ramoth – gilead. The prophets told the King of Israel to go into battle, stating

That the Lord will deliver Ramoth – gilead into the hand of the King (1 Kings 22:6). Jehoshaphat asks if there are any prophets of whom to inquire the word of the Lord. Ahab mentions Micaiah the son of Imiah, but expresses dislike for him because his past prophecies have not been in favour of him (1 Kings 22: 7-8). A messenger is sent to bring Micaiah to the King to give his prophecy. The messenger told Micaiah to give a favourable prophecy to Ahab (1 Kings 22: 12-13)

Micaiah replies to the messenger that he will speak whatever the Lord says to him (1 Kings 22:14).

Micaiah appears before the King of Israel, and when asked if Ahab should go into battle at Ramoth- gilead Micaiah initially responds with a similar prophesy to that of the other prophets. Ahab then questions Micaiah, and insists that he speak nothing but the truth in the name of the Lord. Micaiah then gave a true prophecy, in which he illustrates a meeting of Yahweh with the heavenly hosts. At this meeting Yahweh asks who will entice Ahab to go into battle so that he may perish (1 Kings 22: 19-20).

A spirit comes forward, and offers to "be a lying spirit in the mouth of the prophets" (1 Kings 22: 22).

Therefore, the prophecies of the other prophets were a result of the lying spirit. As a result of this prophesy, Ahab ordered Micaiah imprisoned until he returned from battle, unharmed (1 Kings 22: 27).

Perhaps concerned about prophesy, Ahab disguised himself in battle rather than lead his army openly as their king.

Ahab was killed during the battle after being struck by a randomly shot arrow.

Micaiah's prophecy was fulfilled, contrary to the word of the other 400 false prophets, all of whom encouraged Ahab to attack with a prediction of victory.

Hosea

Hosea and Amos, where the last chance prophets.

Soon the people would be exiled never to return.

Neither Amos of Hosea succeeded in bringing Israel back to God.

God was forced to judge the people and they were taken into Exile in 721 BC.

They both prophesied in the 8th century.

(Rome and Carthage were founded in the 8th Century. Also the Olympic Games began in Greece).

Hosea, son of Beeri, was an 8th century BC Prophet in Israel who authorised the book of prophecies bearing his name. He is one of the twelve prophets of the Bible, also known as Minor Prophets.

Hosea is often seen as the "prophet of doom", but underneath his message of destruction is a promise of restoration.

The period of Hosea's ministry extended to sixty years and he was the only prophet of Israel of his time who left any written prophesy.

Family

Little is known about the life or social status of Hosea. According to the book of Hosea, he married the prostitute Gomer, the daughter of Diblaim, at God's command. In Hosea 5:8, there is a reference to the wars which led to the capture of the Kingdom by the Assyrians (734-732 BC). It is not certain if he experienced the destruction of Samaria, which is foreseen in Hosea 14:1.

Hosea's family life reflected the "adulterous" relationship which Israel had built with polytheistic gods.

The relationship between Hosea and Gomer parallels the relationship between God and Israel. Even though Gomer runs away from Hosea and sleeps with another man, he loves her anyway and forgives her. Likewise, even though the people of Israel worshipped false gods, God continued to love them and did not abandon his covenant with them.

Similarly, his children's names made them like walking prophecies of the fall of the ruling dynasty and the severed covenant with God- much like the prophet Isaiah a generation later. The name of Hosea's daughter, Lo-ruhamah, which translates as "not pitied", is chosen by God as a sign of displeasure with the people of Israel for following false gods. (Hosea 2:23) she is redeemed, shown mercy.

The name of Hosea's son, Lo-Ammi, which translates as "not my people", is chosen by the Lord as a sign of the Lord's displeasure with the people of Israel for following those false gods (Hosea 1: 8-9).

One of the early writing prophets, Hosea used his own experience as a symbolic representation of God and Israel:

God the husband, Israel the wife. Hosea's wife left him to go with other men; Israel left the Lord to go with false gods. Hosea searched for his wife, found her and brought her back; God would not abandon Israel and brought them back even though they had forsaken him.

The book of Hosea was a severe warning to the northern Kingdom against the growing idolatry practiced there; the book was a dramatic call to repentance.

Charles Spurgeon, saw Hosea as a striking presentation of the mercy of God in his sermon on Hosea 1:7 titled "The Lord's own salvation". "But I will have mercy upon the house of Judah, and will save them by the Lord their God, and will not save them by bow, nor by sword, nor by battle, by horse, nor by horsemen. Tomb of Hosea

The Tomb of Hosea is a structure located in the Jewish cemetery of Safed, believed to be the final resting place of Hosea.

Amos

Amos, was another of the Minor Prophets. An older contemporary of Hosea and Isaiah, Amos was active ((760-755 BC), during the reign of Jeroboam 11. He was from the Southern Kingdom of Judah but preached in the northern Kingdom of Israel. Amos wrote at a time of relative peace and prosperity but also spoke of the neglect of Gods laws.

He spoke against an increased disparity between the very wealthy and the very poor.

His major themes of social justice, God's omnipotence, and divine judgement became staples of prophecy. The book of Amos is attributed to him.

Life

Before becoming a prophet, Amos was a sheep herder and a sycamore fig farmer. Amos 'prior professions and his claim "I am not a prophet nor a son of a prophet" 7:14. Indicate that Amos was not from a school of prophets, which Amos claims makes him a true prophet. Amos' declaration marks a turning point in the development of the Old Testament prophesy. It is not mere chance that Hosea, Isaiah, Jeremiah, Ezekiel, and almost all of the prophets who are more than unknown personages to whom a few prophetical speeches are ascribed, give first of all the story of the special calling. All of them thereby seek to protest against the suspicion that they are professional prophets, because the latter discredited themselves by flattering national vanities and ignoring the misdeeds of prominent men.

The home town of Amos was Tekoa, which was 12 miles from Jerusalem in the southern Kingdom.

He had Visions when he was awake and dreams while he slept.

He came with a strong appeal to return to the Lord.

The Bible speaks of his ministry and prophecies concluding around 762, two years before the earthquake that is spoken of in Amos 1:1, "two years before the earthquake". The prophet Zechariah likely was referencing this same earthquake several centuries later. From Zechariah 14:5 "And you shall flee as you fled from the earthquake in the days of Uzziah King of Judah.

Despite being from the southern Kingdom of Judah Amos' prophetic message was aimed at the northern Kingdom of Israel, particularly the cities of Samaria and Bethel.

Jeroboam 11 (781-741 BC) , ruler of the Northern Kingdom, had rapidly conquered Syria, Moab, and Ammon, and extended his dominions from the source of the Orontes on the North to the dead sea on the south. The whole Northern Empire of Solomon was almost restored and was enjoying a long period of peace.

Social corruption and the oppression of the poor and helpless were prevalent.

Amos was the first prophet to write down the messages he had received. He had always been admired for the purity of his language, the beauty of his diction, and his poetic art.

God showed him two pictures: the first showed locusts devouring everything, the second picture showed a fire destroying everything in the city. Amos was shocked and begged God Not to do this, and God drew back from what he said he would do. (Prayer can effect God).

Amos felt himself called to preach in Bethel, where there was a royal sanctuary, and there to announced the fall of the reigning dynasty and of the northern kingdom. But he is denounced by the head priest Amaziah to King Jeroboam 11 and is advised to leave the kingdom. There is no reason to doubt that he was forced to leave the northern kingdom and to return to his native country.

Being thus prevented from bringing his message to an end, and from reaching the ear of those to whom he was sent, he had no recourse to writing. If they could not hear his messages, they could read them, and if his contemporaries refused to do so, following generations might still profit by them. No earlier instance of a literary prophet is known; but the example he gave was followed by others in an almost unbroken succession. It cannot be proved that Hosea knew the book of Amos, though there is no reason to doubt that he was acquainted with the work of Amos. It is certain that Isaiah knew his book, for he follows and even imitates him in his early speeches (compare Amos, V 21-24 et seq., V 18 with Isaiah 11-15;

His last Message was especially fierce. The vision of fruit suggests that Israel is "ripe for judgement".

God says he will never forget them-he records everything, he only forgets what he has forgiven.

Amos tells the people, that the 10 tribes will be scattered among the nations, never to rise again.

The Apocryphal work THE LIVES OF THE PROPHETS records that Amos was killed by the son of Amaziah, priest of Bethel. It further states that before he died, Amos made his way back to his homeland and was buried there.

Jonah

Jonah was a prophet of the northern kingdom of Israel in about the 8th century. He is the central figure in the book of Jonah, famous for being swallowed by a giant fish.

Jonah is the son of Amittai, and he appears in 2 Kings as a prophet from Gath-Hepher, a few miles north of Nazareth. He is therein described as being active during the reign of the second King Jeroboam (786-746 BC), and as predicting that Jeroboam will recover certain lost territories.

Jonah was commanded by God to go to the city of Nineveh to prophesy against it "for their great wickedness is come up before me," Jonah instead seeks to flee from "the presence of the Lord" by going to Joppa, identified now as Jaffa, and sailing to Tarshish, which, is in the opposite direction. A huge storm arises and the sailors, realizing that it was no ordinary storm, cast lots and discover that Jonah is to blame. Jonah admits this and states that if he is thrown overboard, the storm will cease. The sailors try to dump as much cargo as possible before giving up, but feel forced to throw Jonah overboard, at which point the sea calms. The sailors then offer a sacrifice to God. Jonah is miraculously saved by being swallowed by a large fish in whose belly he spends three days and nights. While in the great fish, Jonah prays to God in his affliction and commits to thanksgiving and to paying what he has vowed. God commands the fish to spew Jonah out.

God again commands Jonah to visit Nineveh and prophesy to its inhabitants.

It was 70 miles from his home town near Nazareth to Joppa, about the distance from Bracknell to Bath.

From Joppa to Nineveh was about 670 miles, as far as from Bracknell to the very northerly tip of Scotland.

In the time of Jonah, there was no Cars, trains or aeroplanes.

If a person was lucky they may have a donkey, but as there is no record in the Bible of Jonah having a Donkey, we have to assume that he had to walk, and he may had been in danger of being attacked by robbers.

This time he goes and enters the city, crying "in forty days Nineveh shall be overthrown." After Jonah has walked across Nineveh, the people of Nineveh begin to believe his word and proclaim a fast. The king of Nineveh puts on sackcloth and sits in ashes, making a proclamation which decrees fasting, sackcloth, prayer, and repentance. God sees their repentant hearts and spares the city at that time. The Entire city is humbled and broken with the people (and even the animals) in sackcloth and ashes. Even the king comes off his throne to repent.

Displeased by this, Jonah refers to his earlier flight to Tarshish while asserting that, since God is merciful, it was inevitable that God would turn from the threatened calamities. He then leaves the city and makes himself a shelter, waiting to see whether or not the city will be destroyed. God causes a plant to grow over Jonah's shelter to give him some shade from the sun. Later, God causes a worm to bite the plant's root and it withers. Jonah now being exposed to the full force of the sun, becomes faint and desires that God take him out of the world.

God said to Jonah:" art thou greatly angry for the Kikayon?" and he said "I am greatly angry, even unto death".

And the Lord said "Thou hast pity on the gourd, for which thou hast not laboured, neither made it grow, which came up at night, and perished in a night;

And should not I have pity on Nineveh, that great city, wherein are more than six score thousand persons that cannot discern between their right hand and their left hand, and also much cattle? (Jonah 4:9-11).

(Jonah 3:3) It would take 3 days to walk across the city.

(Jonah 4: 11) 120,000 people lived in the city.

Classic writers wrote it was 60 miles wide.

Nahum later prophesied that the people would be taken into exile, which happened in 612 BC.

Comment: As Jonah seemed to be scared to go to Nineveh with God's prophesy. Could he had sent Gods prophecy to them in a letter like Amos did?

Personally I don't think a letter would had worked.

Jonah walked across the whole city, shouting out God's **Prophesy.**

When he had completed his walk, they believed.

A letter to the king would not have the whole city believing.

A king's order to do things, can't have the same effect, they would do what they were ordered to do, but it would not come from their hearts.

Let's look at Jonah now. He was told by God to go to Nineveh and prophesy, now this could upset the king and lead to Jonah's death.

So he ran away in the opposite direction.

(Is this what we would do?).

Eventually he got the message and went.

The people of Nineveh heard the prophecy and repented. God forgave them.

What was Jonah's reaction? He was not happy at all. He had ran away in a boat, thrown in the sea, eaten by a fish.

Eventually he went to Nineveh. There He delivered God's warning.

Then he leaves the city and just sits and waits to see what God would do.

What did God Do? As we have seen many times, he forgives the people when they repented.

Jonah after all he had gone through, maybe he actually wanted God to punish the people of Nineveh.

Do we ever feel this way?

Someone has wronged us and we want them punished.

They say sorry and really mean it but it is sometimes hard to forgive.

Maybe the person had hurt others not yourself.

For instance someone has shot and killed a lot of people in a night club in Paris.

Do we think the killers should be punished?

We all fall short, even Jonah.

We all need forgiveness, the blood of Jesus and God's grace.

Elijah

Elijah was a prophet who lived in the northern kingdom of Israel during the reign of Ahab 9th century BC.

By the 9th century BC, the Kingdom of Israel, once united under Solomon, was divided into the northern Kingdom of Israel and the southern Kingdom of Judah.

Omri, king of Israel, continued policies dating from the reign of Jeroboam, contrary to religious law , that were intended to reorient religious focus away from Jerusalem: encouraging the building of local temple altars for sacrifices, appointing priests from outside the family of the Levites, and allowing or encouraging temples dedicated to Baal, an important deity in Canaanite religion. Omri achieved domestic security with a marriage alliance between his son Ahab and Princess Jezebel, a princess of Baal and the daughter of the king of Sidon in Phoenicia. These solutions brought security and economic prosperity to Israel for a time, but did not bring peace with the Israelite prophets, who were interested in a strict deuteronomic interpretation of the law.

Under Ahab's kingship, these tensions were exacerbated. Ahab built a temple for Baal, and his wife Jezebel brought a large entourage of priests and prophets of Baal and asherah into the country. It is in this context that Elijah is introduced in 1 Kings 17:1 as Elijah "the Tishbite". He warns Ahab that there will be years of catastrophic drought so severe that not even dew will fall, because Ahab and his queen stand at the end of a line of kings of Israel who said to have "done evil in the sight of the Lord".

Widow of Zarephath

After Elijah's confrontation with Ahab, God tells him to flee out of Israel, to a hiding place by the brook Chorath, east of the Jordan, where he will be fed by Ravens.

When the brook dries up, God sends him to a widow living in the Town of Zarephatho in Phoenicia. When Elijah finds her and asks to be fed, she says that she does not have sufficient food to keep her and her own son alive. Elijah tells her that God will not allow her supply of oil and flour to run out, saying " Don't be afraid , this is what the Lord, the God of Israel, says: " The Jar of flour will not be used up and the jug of oil will not run dry until the day the Lord gives rain on the land". She feeds him the last of her food, and Elijah's promise comes true; thus, by an act of faith the woman received the promised blessing. God gave her" manna" from heaven even while he was withholding food from his unfaithful people in the Promised Land. Sometime later the widow's son dies and the widow cries, "Did you come to remind me of my sin and kill my son?" Moved by a faith like that of Abraham (Romans 4:17, Hebrews 11:19), Elijah prays that God might restore her son so that the veracity and trustworthiness of God's word might be demonstrated. 1 Kings 17:22 relates God "heard the voice of Elijah; and the soul of the child came into him again, and he revived. "This is the first instance of raising the dead recorded in scripture. The woman cried "the word of the Lord from your mouth is the truth. "She made a confession that the Israelites had failed to make.

After three more years of drought and famine, God tells Elijah to return to Ahab and announce the end of the drought: not occasioned by repentance in Israel but by the command of the Lord, who had determined to reveal himself to his people. While on his way, Elijah meets Obadiah, the head of Ahab's household, who had hidden a hundred prophets of Yahweh when Ahab and Jezebel had been killing them. Elijah sends Obadiah back to Ahab to announce his return to Israel.

Challenge to Baal

When Ahab confronts Elijah, he refers to him as the "troubler of Israel". Elijah responds by throwing the charge back at Ahab, saying that it is Ahab who has troubled Israel by allowing the worship of false gods. Elijah then berates both the people of Israel and Ahab for worshipping Baal.

"If the Lord is God, follow him; but if Baal is then follow him" I Kings 18:21. And the people were silent.

At this point Elijah proposes a direct test of the powers of Baal and Yahweh. The people of Israel, 450 prophets of Baal, and 400 prophets of asherah are summoned to Mount Carmel. Two alters are built, one for Baal and one for Yahweh. Wood is laid on the altars. Two Oxen are slaughtered and cut into pieces; the pieces are laid on the wood. Elijah then invites the priests of Baal to pray for fire to light the sacrifice, they pray from morning to noon without success.

Elijah ridicules their efforts. "And it came to pass at noon, that Elijah mocked them, and said, cry aloud for he is a God, either he is talking, or pursuing, or he is in a journey, or peradventure, and must be awaked". (1 Kings 18:27) They responded by cutting themselves and adding their own blood to the sacrifice (such mutilation of the body was forbidden under Mosaic Law). They continued praying until evening without success.

Elijah now orders the Altar of Yahweh be drenched with water from "four large jars" poured three times (1 Kings 18:33-34). He asks God to accept the sacrifice. Fire falls from the sky, consuming the water, the sacrifice and the stones itself as well. Elijah then orders the death of the prophets of Baal. Elijah prays earnestly for rain to fall again on the land. Then the rains begin, signalling the end of the famine.

Mount Horeb

Jezebel, enraged that Elijah had ordered the death of her priests, threatens to kill Elijah (1 Kings 19: 1-13). Later Elijah would prophesy about Jezebel's death, because of her sin. Later, Elijah flees to Beersheba in Judah, continues alone in the wilderness, and finally sits down under a Retamaine shrub, praying for death. He falls asleep under the tree, the

Angel of the Lord touches him and tells him to wake up and eat. When he awakes he finds bread and a jar of water. He eats, drinks, and goes back to sleep. The Angel comes a second time and tells him to eat and drink because he has a long journey ahead of him.

Elijah travels (walks) for 40 days and 40 nights to Mount Horeb, where Moses had received the Ten Commandments. Elijah is the only person described in the Bible as returning to Horeb, after Moses and his generation had left Horeb several centuries before. He seeks shelter in a cave. God again speaks to Elijah (1 Kings 19:9). "What does thou here Elijah?" Elijah did not give a direct answer to the Lord's question but evades and equivocates, implying that the work of the Lord had begun centuries earlier had now come to nothing, and that his own work was fruitless. Unlike Moses, who tried to defend Israel when they sinned with the golden calf, Elijah bitterly complains over the Israelites' unfaithfulness and says he is the "only one left". Up until this time Elijah has only the word of God to guide him, but now he is told to go outside the cave and "stand before the Lord." A terrible wind passes, but God is not in the wing. A great earthquake shakes the mountain, but God is not in the earthquake. Then a fire passes the mountain, but God is not in the fire. Then a "still small voice" comes to Elijah and asks again, "What does thou here, Elijah?" Elijah again evades the question and his lament is unrevised, showing that he did not understand the importance of the divine revelation he had just witnessed. God then sends him out again, this time to Damascus to anoint Hazael as King of Syria, Jehi as King of Israel, and Elisha as his replacement.

(It is believed that Mount Horeb and Mount Sinai are the same Mountain. Some people believe that one side is Sinai, the other side is Horeb.)

Vineyard of Naboth

Elijah encounters Ahab again in 1 Kings 21, after Ahab had acquired possession of a Vineyard by murder. Ahab to have the vineyard of Naboth of Jezreel. He offers a better vineyard or a fair price for the land. But Naboth tells Ahab that God has told him not to part with the land. Ahab accepts this answer with a sullen bad grace. Jezebel, however, plots a method for acquiring the land. She sends letters, in Ahab's name, to the elders and nobles who lived near Naboth. They are to arrange a feast and invite Naboth. At the feast, false charges of cursing God or Ahab are to be made against him. The plot is carried out and Naboth is stoned to death. When word comes that Naboth is dead, Jezebel tells Ahab to take possession of the vineyard.

God again speaks to Elijah and sends him to confront Ahab with a question and a prophesy; "have you killed Naboth and also taken possession of his land? "So I will tell you this, in the same place where dogs licked up the blood of Naboth, shall dogs lick up your own blood" (1 Kings 21:19).

Ahab begins the confrontation by calling Elijah his enemy. Elijah responds by throwing the charge back at him, telling him that he has made himself the enemy of God by his own actions. Elijah then goes beyond the prophesy he was given and tells Ahab that his entire kingdom will reject his authority; that Jezebel will be eaten by dogs within Jezreel; and that his family will be consumed by dogs as well (if they die in the city) or the birds(if they die in the country).

When Ahab hears this he repents to such a degree that God relents in punishing Ahab but will punish Jezebel and their son (Ahaziah).

Ahaziah

Elijah continues now from Ahab to an encounter with Ahaziah. The scene opens with Ahaziah seriously injured in a fall. He sends to the priests of Baalzebub in Ekron, outside the kingdom of Israel, to know if he will recover. Elijah intercepts his messengers and sends them back to Ahaziah with a message "it is because there is no God in Israel that you are sending to inquire of Baalzebub, the god of Ekron?? " (2 Kings 1:6). Ahaziah asks the messengers to describe the person who gave them this message. They tell him he was a hairy man with a leather girth round his loin and he instantly recognizes the description as Elijah the Tishbite.

Ahaziah sends out three groups of soldiers to arrest Elijah. The first two are destroyed by fire which Elijah calls down from Heaven. The leader of the third group asks for mercy for himself and his men. Elijah agrees to accompany this third group to Ahaziah, where he gives his prophecy in person.

Departure

Elijah, in company with Elisha, approaches the Jordan. He rolls up his mantle and strikes the water (2 Kings 2:8). The water immediately divides and Elijah and Elisha cross on dry land, suddenly, a chariot of fire and horses of fire appear and Elijah is lifted up in a whirlwind. As Elijah is lifted up, his mantle falls to the ground and Elisha picks it up.

Final Mention

Elijah is mentioned once more in 2 Chronicles 21:12, which will be his final mention. A letter is sent under the Prophet's name to Jeroboam of Judah. It tells him that he has led the people of Judah astray.

The Prophet ends the letter with a prediction of a painful death. This letter is a puzzle to readers for several reasons. First, it concerns a king of the southern kingdom, while Elijah concerned himself with the kingdom of Israel. Second, the message begins with "thus says YHVH, God of your father David" rather than the more usual" in the name of YHVH the God of Israel." Also, this letter seems to come after Elijah's ascension into the whirlwind.

Remember Amos wrote his Prophecy and sent it to the King.

In the Book of Malachi, it prophesises a Messiah.

It is written, "Behold, I will send you Elijah the Prophet before the coming of the great and terrible day of the Lord". That day is described as the burning of a great furnace," so that it will leave them neither root nor branch." (Malachi 3:19).

The final verses in Malachi are believed to indicate that Elijah has a role in the end of times, immediately before the second coming of Jesus.

Elisha

Elisha, was a disciple of Elijah and, after Elijah was taken up into the whirlwind, Elisha was accepted as the leader of the sons of the prophets.

Elisha's story is related in the Book of Kings. He was active during the reign of Joram, Jehu, Jehoahaz, and Jehoash.

Elisha was the son of Shaphat, a wealthy land owner of Abel- meholah.

His name first occurs in the command given to Elijah to anoint him as his successor. After learning in the cave on mount Horeb, that Elisha, the son of Shaphat, had been selected by Yahweh as his successor in the prophetic office, Elijah set out to find him. On the way from Sinai to Damascus, Elijah found Elisha "one of them that were ploughing with twelve yoke of Oxen." Elisha delayed only long enough to Kill the oxen, and boil their flesh with the wood of the plough. He went over to him, threw his mantle over Elisha's shoulders, and at once adopted him as a son, investing him with the Prophetic office.

Elisha accepted his call about four years before the death of Israel's King Ahab.

For the next seven or eight years Elisha became Elijah's close attendant until Elijah was taken up into heaven.

Before Elijah was taken up into the Whirlwind, Elisha asked to "inherit a double -portion" of Elijah's spirit. Some scholars see this as indicative of the property inheritance customs of the time, where the eldest son received twice as much of the father's inheritance as each of the youngest sons. In this interpretation Elisha is asking that he may be seen as the "rightful heir" and successor to Elijah.

By means of the Mantle let fall from Elijah, Elisha miraculously re crossed the Jordan, and Elisha returned to Jericho, where he won gratitude of the people by purifying the unwholesome waters of their spring and making them drinkable.

Before he settled in Samaria, Elisha passed some time on Mount Carmel. When the armies of Judah, Israel, and Edom, then allied against Mesha, the Moabite king, were being tortured by drought in the Idumean desert, Elisha consented to intervene. His double prediction regarding relief from drought and victory over the Moabites was fulfilled on the following morning. When a group of boys from Bethel taunted the prophet for his baldness, Elisha cursed them in the name of Yahweh and two female bears came out of the forest and tore forty two of the boys apart.

Elisha became noted in Israel, and for six decades (892-832BC) held the office of "prophet in Israel". He is termed a Patriot, as he was involved in helping soldiers and kings.

Wonder Worker

To relieve the widow importuned by a hard creditor, Elisha so multiplied a little oil as to enable her, not only to pay her debt, but to provide for her family needs. To reward the rich lady of Shunem for her hospitality, he obtained for her from Yahweh, at first the birth of a son, and subsequently the resurrection of her child, who had died.

To nourish the sons of the prophet pressed by famine, Elisha changed into wholesome food the pottage made from poisonous gourds.

Elisha cured the Syrian military commander Naaman of leprosy but punished his own servant Gehazi, who took money from Naaman.

Naaman, at first reluctant, obeyed Elisha, and washed 7 times in the Jordan. Finding his flesh "restored like the flesh of a child", the general was so impressed by this evidence of Gods power, and by the disinterestedness of his prophet, as to express his deep conviction that "there is no other God in all the Earth, but only in Israel".

Elisha's public political actions included repeatedly saving King Jehoram of Israel from the ambushes planned by Benhadad, ordering the elders to shut the door against the messenger of Israel's ungrateful King, bewildering with a strange blindness the soldiers of the Syrian King, making iron float to relieve from embarrassment a son of a prophet, confidently predicting the sudden flight of the enemy and the consequent cessation of the famine, and unmasking the treachery of Hazael.

Other miracles Elisha accomplishes include multiplying loaves of new barley into a sufficient supply for a hundred men, and for a disciple of the schools of the prophets, he recovers an axe fallen into the waters of the Jordan. He administered the miracle at Dothan, half way on the road between Samaria and Jezreel, and at the siege of Samaria by the King of Syria, Elisha prophesied about the terrible sufferings of the people of Samaria and their eventual relief.

Elisha then journeyed to Damascus and prophesied that Hazael would be King over Syria, thereafter he directs one of the sons of the prophets to anoint Jehu, son of Jehoshapat, King of Israel, in place of Ahab. Mindful of the order given by Elijah, Elisha delegated a son of one of the prophets to quietly anoint Jehu King of Israel, and to commission him to cut off the house of Ahab. The Death of Jehoram, pierced by an arrow from Jehu's bow, the ignominious end of Jezebel, the slaughter of Ahab's seventy sons, proved how faithfully executed was the Divine command. After predicting to Jehoash his victory over the Syrians at Aphek, as well as three other victories, ever bold before Kings, ever kindly towards the lowly, "Elisha died, and they buried him".

While Elisha lay on his death bed in his house, Jehoash, the grandson of Jehu, came to mourn over his approaching departure, and uttered the same words as those of Elisha when Elijah was taken away, indicating his value to him " My father, my father! The chariot of Israel, and the horsemen there of."

A year after Elisha's death and burial a body was placed in his grave.

As soon as the body touched Elisha's bones the man "revived, and stood up on his feet". It has been said, that this dead man was Shallum (son of Tikvah), keeper of the temple Wardrobe in the reign of Josiah and husband of Huldah the prophetess.

Oded

Oded was a prophet of the Lord. He went out to meet the army that came to Samaria and said to them, "behold, because the Lord, the God of your fathers, was angry with Judah, he gave them into your hand, but you have killed them in a rage that has reached up to heaven. (2 Chronicles 28:9).

He was only a minor prophet but needed to be mentioned.

Chapter Five - Prophets of Judah: Hanani to Habakkuk

Hanani

The Prophet Hanani, was sent to rebuke King Asa of Judah for entering into a league with Benhadad 1, King of Syria, against the Northern Kingdom of Israel(2 Chr. 16:1-10). This Hanani was also probable the father of the prophet Jehu (1 Kings 16:7).

Jehu

The Prophet Jehu, condemned Baasha, King of Israel, "and his house" (1 Kings 16:7), accusing him of leading the people into the sin of idolatry like his predecessor Jeroboam. Jehu's words were fulfilled in the reign of Elah, Baasha's son, when the traitor Zimri assassinated Elah and murdered all of Baasha's family and associates. (1 Kings 16: 1, 7, 12,).

Jehu also challenged Jehoshaphat, king of Judah. Jehoshaphat's alliance with Ahab ended in the latter's death at the battle of Ramoth-Gilead. Jehoshaphat returned safely, but Jehu rebuked him for helping the wicked king Ahab. He went on to say that nevertheless the Lord found good in the king, as he had removed the Asherah poles from the land and set his heart to seek God (2 Chronicles 19:2-3).

Jahaziel

Jahaziel, a Levite, is mentioned as delivering a divine message.

2 Chronicles 20, recounts a joint attack on Judah by the nations of Moab, Ammon, and Edom in the time of King Jehoshaphat.

The King declared a fast to the Lord and prayed for his help before the assembled nation.

"Then in the mist of the congregation the spirit of the Lord came upon Jahaziel son of Zechariah, and he said," give heed, all Judah and the inhabitants of Jerusalem and king Jehoshaphat; thus said the Lord to you, " do not fear or be dismayed by this great multitude, for the battle is God's, not yours(1 Chronicles 20:14-15). The next morning, Jehosaphat led his people out, calling them to have faith in the Lord, and leading them in praise. They saw their enemies turn on each other, and returned to Jerusalem in Joy. After that the kingdom of Judah was at peace thanks to divine intervention against their enemies.

Eliezer

Eliezer is a Minor prophet in the bible who only made an appearance in 2 Chronicles 20:37. His father was named Dodovahu, who is also an unknown biblical figure.

Eliezer is the only person mentioned in the bible who was a prophet. He appears on the Biblical Timeline Chart with

World History during the reign of King Jehoshaphat around 925BC.

Obadiah

Obadiah's prophecy, directed against Edom, presupposes that a looting of Jerusalem and a carrying away of many Jews into captivity had recently taken place. Some believe that the prophet refers to the conquest of Jerusalem at the time of King Jehoram (2 Kings 8: 20-22); (Chronicles 21:8-10), in the 9th century; others believe that the

Prophet is speaking of Jerusalem's destruction by Nebuchadnezzar in 586 BC.

In the Epistle to the Hebrews, Christians are told not to be like Esau, who sold his birth right for a bowl of stew, then wept after. He was full of regret and remorse, but he was never able to repent.

Instead we are told to be more like a Jacob. He wrestled with God until God made him limp, but he got the blessing, and it is from Jacob that God's people Israel came. Esau lived for the present and lost his future.

The Book of Obadiah encourages us to be a Jacob- the man who was broken by God and became a prince.

Jahaziel

2 Chronicles 20 recounts a joint attack on Judah by the nations of Moab, Ammon, and Edom in the time of King Jehoshaphat. The King declared a fast to the Lord and prayed for his help before the assembled nation. "then in the midst of the congregation the spirit of the Lord came upon Jahaziel son of Zechariah, and he said, " give heed, all Judah and the inhabitants of Jerusalem and King Jehoshaphat; thus said the Lord to you, " Do not fear or be dismayed by this great multitude, for the battle is God's, not yours."

The next morning, Jehosaphat led his people out, calling them to have faith in the Lord. They saw their enemy's turn on each other.

Joel

Joel, was a prophet of Israel, the second of the 12 Minor Prophets.

The son of Pethuel (Joel 1:1).

The Dates of his life are unknown; he may have lived anywhere from the 9th century to the 5th century BC, depending on the dating of his book.

The book's mention of Greeks has not given scholars any help in dating the text since the Greeks were known to have access to Judah from Mycenaean times (1600-1100BC). However, the book's mention of Judah's suffering and to the standing Temple, has led some scholars to place the date of the book in the post-exile period, after the construction of the second temple.

Joel was originally from Judah/Judea, and, judging from its prominence in his prophesy, was quite possible a prophet associated with the ritual of Solomon's or even the second temple.

According to a long standing tradition, Joel was buried in Gush Halav.

Amoz

Amoz was the father of the Prophet Isaiah. Nothing else is known about him. There is a Talmudic tradition that when the name of a prophet's father is given, the father was also a prophet, so that Amoz would had been a prophet like his son.

Though it is mentioned frequently as the patronymic title of Isaiah, the name Amoz appears nowhere else in the Bible.

Isaiah

Isaiah, was an 8th century prophet.

The call of Isaiah gives us an unexpected reference to the Trinity.

Isaiah was asked by God, "Whom shall I send? And who will go for us"? (US is the plural).

It is believed that the book of Isaiah all 66 chapters was written by Isaiah. Some people believe the book was written by two or even three Isaiah's, but as we only know of the death of one Isaiah, then it is most believable that there was only one Isaiah.

This was written in possibly two periods between 740 BC and 686BC.

A gap of approximately 15 years, and includes dramatic prophetic declarations of Cyrus the Great in the Bible, acting to restore the nation of Israel from exile in Babylon.

The first verse of the book of Isaiah states that Isaiah prophesied during the reigns of Uzziah, Jotham, Ahaz and Hezekiah, the kings of Judah (Isaiah 1:1).

Uzziah reign was 52 years in the middle of the 8th century BCE, and Isaiah must have begun his ministry a few years before Uzziah's death. Probably in the 740's BC. Isaiah lived until the fourteenth year of Hezekiah's reign (who died 698 BC). He may also had been contemporary for some years with Manasseh. Thus Isaiah may have for as long as 64 years.

King Manasseh, was a very bad king, involved in Devil worship, even sacrificed his own son to the demonic god molech, who was the centre of satanic worship in Judah.

According to some modern interpretations Isaiah's wife was called "The prophetess", either because she was endowed with the prophetic gift, like Deborah (Judges 4:4), or simply because she was the "wife of the prophet" (as he is named, in this case Isaiah).

They had two sons, named She'ar-Yashuv, and the younger, Maher-Shalal-Hash-Baz,

Soon after this, Shalmaneser V determined to subdue the Kingdom of Israel, Samaria was taken and destroyed (722BCE).So long as Ahaz reigned, the Kingdom of Judah was unmolested by the Assyrians; but on his accession to the throne, Hezekiah, was encouraged to rebel against Assyria (2 Kings 18:7), he entered into an alliance with the king of Egypt (Isaiah 30:2-4). This led to the king of Assyria to threaten the king of Judah, and eventually to invade. Sennacherib (701BC) led a large army into Judah. Hezekiah was petrified, and submitted to the Assyrians (2 Kings 18:14-16). But after a short time war broke out again. Again Sennacherib led an army into Judah, one section of the Assyrian army threatened Jerusalem (Isaiah 36:2-22).

Isaiah on this occasion encouraged Hezekiah to resist the Assyrians. The Sennacherib sent a threatening letter to Hezekiah, which he "spread before the Lord (37:14).

The Judgement of God now fell on the Assyrian army and wiped out 185.000 of its men. "Like Xerxes in Greece, Sennacherib never recovered from the shock of the disaster in Judah.

The remaining years of Hezekiah's reign were peaceful (2 Chronicles 32:23-29). Isaiah probable lived to its close.

The Talmud (Yevamot 49b) says that Manasseh became very angry with Isaiah, and devised a painful death for him.

Many painful ways of killing people have been devised over the centuries, but I think Isaiah was the only man to die this way.

Isaiah was tied up, then put inside the trunk of a tree, then two of the kings woodsmen took a saw and cut through the tree about the centre of where Isaiah was encased.

The book of Isaiah is quoted many times by New Testament writers. Ten of those references are about the Suffering Servant, how he will suffer and die to save many from their sins, be buried in a rich man's tomb, be a light to the Gentiles. The Gospel of John even says that Isaiah "saw Jesus" glory and spoke about him.

In the Book of Isaiah, there are many verses predicting the birth of Jesus.

Zedekiah, was the last king of Judah. When the Babylonians conquered Jerusalem, they dragged Zedekiah out into the street. They bound him up, then killed his children before him.

Before cutting his eyes out.

Micah

Micah was a prophet who came from Shephelah, a poor region of hills 20 miles inland on a 3,000 metre shelf.

He lived between the Philistines and the Jews.

Micah preached at the same time as Isaiah.

Micah reminds us that we should leave the work to God. We must reflect God but our job today is "to act justly, love mercy and walk humbly before our God."

Micah's ministry fell in the reign of King's Jotham, Ahaz, and Hezekiah (Chapter 1:1).

Jeremiah (Chapter 26:18), Quoting Micah (chapter 3:12) testifies that Micah ministered during Hezekiah's reign. This leads to the conclusion that Micah prophesied from about 740 to about 700BC.

Nahum

Nathum, was a Minor prophet. His book comes in chronicle order between Micah and Habakkuk in the bible. He wrote about the end of the Assyrian empire, and its capital city, Nineveh, in a vivid poetic style.

Little is known about Nahum's personal history. His name means "comforter", and he was from the town of Alqosh (Nahum 1:1).

He was a very nationalistic Hebrew, however, and lived among the Elkosshites in peace.

Nahum is the seventh of the Minor Prophets.

Works of Nahum

Nahum's writings could be described as prophesy or history. One account suggests that his writings are prophesy written in about 615 BC, just before the downfall of Assyria. While another account suggests that he wrote this passage as liturgy just after its downfall in 612BC.

Nahum told the Assyrians that they were finished.

The difference between Jonah and Nahum is that on this occasion, God did not let them off.

While God's anger is simmering, it can be turned aside, but when it boils over, nothing can stop it.

The king of Nineveh fasted and prayed like in the time of Jonah, but this time God's anger was boiling and his repentance was too late.

The last verse of Nahum has the stern words "there is no remedy for your wounds; your injury is past healing.

Nineveh today

Nineveh as God decreed was totally destroyed.

The City which stood near Modern day Mosul, was surveyed by Claudius J Rich in 1820.

Archaeologist have dug up many things including, the temple of Nabu, The palace of Sennacherib and the Palace of Ashumasirpal.

Comment

God's Anger is like when we boil an egg.

We first pour cold water in a saucepan (this is no anger), add the egg.

Then we turn the Gas on and the water gets Hot (This is anger starting), after a while the water is simmering, (this is the point when God's anger can be stopped with repentance).

We see the simmering water, then slip into the next room for something. (While we are away the water boils, we rush back to the saucepan but it's too late the water is boiling over, we turn the gas off but it's too late).

Remember when God's anger is simmering, it can be stopped but when it boils, it can't be stopped.

A couple of days after researching this, I was driving my car along the road when I was approaching a one way system.

I had right of way and I was nearly at the entrance when another car started coming towards me,(At this point my anger was warming up, I shouted " it's my right of way").

As the driver of the car passed my car, another car started to drive towards me (now my anger was simmering, Again I shouted "it's my right of way")

The car stopped beside my car, the driver a young woman, wound her window down and said "I am sorry". At this point my anger went straight down to cold. (That's how God's anger works).

Neriah.

Neriah, is another prophet, who is only mentioned a couple of times in the Bible.

He was the son of Mahsieah, as well as the father of Baruch and Seraiah ben Neriah, mentioned in the book of Jeremiah (32:12 and 51:59).

Urijah

Urijah, is a prophet mentioned in Jeremiah 26:20-23. He is described as being the son of Shemaiah from Kirjath- jearim. During the reign of Jehoiakim, king of Judah, he fled into Egypt from the cruelty of the king, but having been brought back he was beheaded and his body" cast into the graves of the common people".

Another prophet that we know very little about.

And like most prophets he came to a bad end.

Jeremiah

Jeremiah, also known as the weeping prophet. He was one of the Major Prophets in the Bible.

He began preaching in the seventh century BC.

Almost at the end of the life of the two tribes in the south, who went into exile in 586 BC.

Jeremiah was born at Anathoth (modern Anatah), two miles from Jerusalem. He had to move to Jerusalem, because his family were going to kill him.

He advised the people to surrender to the Babylonians, and the people hated him for this.

He started to speak after the ten tribes of the north had been taken into exile.

Isaiah and Micah had gone, their message largely unheeded.

He was born in the reign of the Evil King Manasseh, the evil King who had Isaiah put to death.

According to religious tradition, he wrote the Book of Jeremiah, Kings and Lamentations, with the assistance of Baruch Ben Neriah, his scribe and assistant.

Greater detail in known about Jeremiah's life than for most of any other prophet. However no biography of him can be written as there are so few facts available.

In Chapter 18, God tells him to visit the potter's house and watch him as he makes his pots depending on the clay at his disposal.

The message Jeremiah picked up was that he saw the potter's intention to make a beautiful vase or pot, but because the clay would not run in his hands, he put it back into a lump, then threw it on the wheel again, and made a thick crude pot.

God asked Jeremiah if he had learned the lesson who decided what the clay would become. The answer is that the clay decides, because it wouldn't run with the potter's original intentions. So the message was that God wanted to make the clay into a beautiful shape, but if the clay would not respond, he would make an ugly shape in the end.

Jeremiah's ministry was active from the thirteenth year of Josiah, King of Judah (3298 AM,) or 626 BC. Until after the fall of Jerusalem and the destruction of Solomon's Temple in 335BC or 287BC.

This period spanned the reigns Jehoahaz, Johoiakim, Jehoiachin, and Zedekiah.

Lineage and early life

Jeremiah was the son of Hilkiah, a Jewish priest from the Benjamite village of Anathoth.

Jeremiah was called to prophetic ministry in. 626BC.

Jeremiah was called by YAHWEH to give prophesy of Jerusalem's destruction that would occur by invaders from the north.

This was because once again Israel had been unfaithful to the laws of the covenant and had forsaken God by worshiping Baal's.

The people of Israel had even gone as far as building high Altars to Baal in order to burn their children in fire as offerings.

This nation had deviated so far from God that they had broken the covenant, causing God to withdraw his blessings.

(Do the Israelites ever learn, how many times in their history have they done this, and been punished, then they repented and were forgiven.)(We are taught that God is our father, what an amazing love our father has).

Jeremiah was guided by God to proclaim that the nation of Judah would be faced with famine, plundered and taken captive by foreigners who would exile them to a foreign land.

(Well we can't be surprised can we, burning their own children as a sacrifice to Baal).

Jeremiah was said to have been appointed to reveal the sins of the people and the coming consequences.

Jeremiah resisted the call by complaining that he was only a child and did not know how to speak.

However, the Lord insisted that Jeremiah go and speak, and he touched Jeremiah's mouth to place the words of the Lord there. God told Jeremiah to "Get yourself ready! The Character traits and practices Jeremiah was to acquire a specified in Jeremiah 1 and includes not being afraid, standing up to speak, speaking as told, and going where sent. Since Jeremiah is described as emerging well trained and fully literate from his earliest preaching, the relationship between him and the Shaphan family has been used to suggest that he may have trained at the tribal school in Jerusalem over which Shaphan presided.

In his early ministry, Jeremiah was primarily a preaching prophet, preaching throughout Israel. He condemned Idolatry, the greed of priests, and false prophets. Many years later, God instructed Jeremiah to write down these oracles and his other messages.

Persecution

Jeremiah's ministry prompted plots against him. (Jer 11:21-23) Unhappy with Jeremiah's message, possibly for concern that it would shut down the Anathoth sanctuary, his priestly kin and the men of Anathoth conspired to kill him. However, the Lord revealed the conspiracy to Jeremiah, protected his life, and declared disaster for the men of Anathoth. When Jeremiah complains to the Lord about this persecution, he is told that the attacks on him will get worse.

A priest Pashur the son of Ben Immer, a temple official in Jerusalem had Jeremiah beaten and put in the stocks at the upper gate of Benjamin for a day. After this, Jeremiah expresses lament over the difficulty that speaking God's word has caused him and regrets becoming a laughingstock and the target of mockery. He recounts how if he tries to shut the word of the Lord inside and not mention God's name, the word becomes like fire in his heart and he is unable to hold it in.

Conflicts with false prophets

Whilst Jeremiah was prophesying the coming destruction, a number of the other prophets were prophesying peace. Jeremiah spoke against these other prophets.

According to the book of Jeremiah, during the reign of King Zedekiah, The Lord instructed Jeremiah to make a yoke of the message that the nation would be subject to the King of Babylon.

The Prophet Hananiah opposed Jeremiah's message. He took the yoke off Jeremiah's neck, broke it, and prophesied to the priests and all the people that within two years the Lord would break the yoke of the King of Babylon, but the Lord spoke to Jeremiah saying "go and speak to Hananiah saying, you have broken the yoke of wood, but you have made instead a yoke of iron" (Jeremiah 28:13).

Relationship with the Northern Kingdom

Jeremiah was sympathetic to as well as descended from the Northern Kingdom. Many of his first reported oracles are about, and addressed to, the Israelites of Samaria. He resembles the northern prophet Hosea, in his use of language, and examples of God's relationship with Israel. Hosea seems to have been the first prophet to describe the desired relationship as an example of ancient Israelite marriage, where a man might be polygamous, while a woman was only permitted one husband. Jeremiah often repeats Hosea's marital imagery (Jer 2:2b-3; 3: 1-5; 4:1-2).

Acting

Sometimes Jeremiah's message was delivered through drama in order to provoke comment. On one occasion he buried some dirty underwear, when asked why, he replied that the underwear depicted the inner lives of the people.

Babylon

The Bible reads that Jeremiah was subjected to more persecutions. After Jeremiah prophesied that Jerusalem would be handed over to the Babylonian army, the King's officials, including Pashur the priest, tried to convince King Zedekiah that Jeremiah should be put to death because he was discouraging his soldiers as well as the people. The King answered that he would not oppose them. Consequently, the King's officials took Jeremiah and put him down into a cistern, where he sunk down into the mud. The intent was to kill Jeremiah by allowing him to starve to death in a manner designed to allow the officials to claim to be innocent of his blood.

(These people are really cunning. But they, like ourselves, forget God is watching us).

A Cushite rescued Jeremiah by pulling him out of the Cistern, but Jeremiah remained imprisoned until Jerusalem fell to the Babylonian army in 586BC.

The Babylonians released Jeremiah, and showed him great kindness, allowing Jeremiah to choose where he wanted to live, according to Babylonian edict. Jeremiah according went to Mizpah in Benjamin with Gedaliah, who had been made governor of Judea.

Egypt

Gedaliah was assassinated by an Israelite prince in the pay of Ammon "for working with the Babylonians". Refusing to listen to Jeremiah's counsel, Johanan fled to Egypt, taking with him Jeremiah and Baruch, and the King's daughters.

While in Egypt, some Jews kidnapped Jeremiah, and took him to Elephantine Island, where the Arc of the covenant had been taken. (This is probably now in Ethiopia). This is where he died, alone, it is a sad story.

Zephaniah

Zephaniah, is the son of Cushi, and great, great grandson of King Hezekiah, ninth in the literary order of the Minor Prophets. He Prophesied in the days of Josiah, King of Judah (BC 641-610), and whom he had much in common.

He is the only Prophet to trace his ancestry back four generations. Hezekiah, the last good King of Judah (Isaiah 36-39), was his great grandfather.

During Manasseh's reign, royal babies were being sacrificed to the god Molech, so it is a theory that Zephaniah was hidden by his mother.

The Scene of his activity was the city of Jerusalem. (Zeph 1:4-10; 3:1, 14).

Under the two previous kings of Judah, Amon and Manasseh, the cult of other deities (especially Baal and Astarte) had developed in the Holy city, bringing with it elements of alien culture and morals.

(Now where have we heard this before? Was it way way back in the time of Lot, a couple of cities called Sodom and Gomorra, These people just don't learn.) (But do we?)

Zephaniah predicted that God would destroy Assyria and make its capital Nineveh absolute wasteland. The once proud city would become a pastureland for sheep and wild animals.

Josiah, a dedicated reformer, wished to put an end to perceived misuse of the Holy places. One of the most Zealous champions and advisers of this reform was Zephaniah, and his writing remains one of the most important documents for the understanding of the era of Josiah.

The prophet spoke boldly against the religious and moral corruption, when, in view of the idolatry which had penetrated even into the sanctuary, he warned that God would "destroy out of this place the remnant of Baal, and the names of the priests" (Zeph 1:4), and pleaded for a return to the simplicity of their fathers instead of the luxurious foreign clothing which was worn especially in aristocratic circles.

The Age of Zephaniah was also a key historical period, because the land of anterior Asia were overrun by foreigners due to the migration of the Scythians in the last decades of the seventh century, and because Jerusalem was only a few decades before its downfall in 586. The light of these events, a message of impending judgement is the primary burden of this figure's preaching.

The Book of Zephaniah

This book contains the fundamental ideas of his preaching.

The Theme of the book in its form is as follows:

Warnings about the "day of the Lord"

Not only Jerusalem, but the entire world is subject to judgement.

(That's saying not only the Jews but all of us Gentiles will be judged one day, we all need to get our acts together).

(Thank God for Jesus. Ephesians 1:7 In Christ we have redemption through his blood, the forgiveness of sins, in accordance with the riches of God's grace.)

The Prophet focuses mostly on Jerusalem.

He gives a prophetic glance at the Kingdom of God of the future.

In the time of Zephaniah, the prophet was certain that God's anger is simmering now, and the day of wrath will come.

God is the father of his people, and a good father disciplines his children when they go wrong. Hebrew's 12 says "if the Lord doesn't discipline you, then you are not a true son of God".

If you become a son of God, then God will discipline you when you sin. God does this so that you won't need to be punished after death.

Habakkuk

Habakkuk, is the author of this book of his name.

He is the eighth of the Minor Prophets.

Habakkuk prophesied around 600 BC.

Habakkuk was a man who clung to God. He also dared to argue with God.

His book is full of "Quotable Quotes" for example.

"Your eyes are to pure to look on evil (1:13)

"In wrath, remember mercy"

"The just shall live by faith"

Almost nothing is known about Habakkuk, apart from a few facts are stated in the book of the Bible bearing his name, or those inferences that may be drawn from the book. His name appears in the Bible only in Habakkuk 1:1 and 3:1, with no biographical details provided other than his title "the Prophet".

Because the book of Habakkuk consists of five oracles about the Chaldeans (Babylonians), and the Chaldean rise to power is dated circa 612 BC, it is assumed he was active about that time, making him an early contemporary of Jeremiah and Zephaniah. Jewish sources, do not group him with those two prophets, who are often placed together, so it is possible that he was slightly earlier than the pair.

Habakkuk is unusual among the prophets in that he openly questions the working of God (1:3a, 1: 13b).

In the first part of the first chapter, the prophet sees the injustice among his people and asks why God does not take action: "1:2 Yahweh, how long will I cry, and you will not hear? I cry out to you 'Violence!' and will you not save?"

It was while he was quiet that Habakkuk saw the light, he stopped arguing with God and thought about what God had said, and his whole mood changed.

He finally understood that God had a much greater picture than he did.

Chapter Six - The Captive Prophets: Daniel to Seraiah

Daniel

The Best way to look at the Prophet Daniel is through the book which he wrote.

Daniel was one of the Major Prophets.

Daniel was born about 622BC, in or near Jerusalem.

In the Reign of Josiah.

Daniels Father was an aristocrat, from the tribe of Judah.

Daniels Father and Mother were believers.

They Led Daniel to the Lord at an early age, when he was a spiritually aware believer.

The Book is divided into two parts

The First Part, Chapters 1-6 is written in the third person, and in Aramaic.

The Second part Chapters 7-12, is written in the singular and in Hebrew.

It appears that Daniel was writing the second part to the Jews.

The Book is set in Babylon (Iraq), in the Reign of Nebuchadnezzar.

Nebuchadnezzar had conquered Assyria, and now wanted to conquer Egypt.

The Problem as always is that Judah was in his way.

So Judah had to be conquered first.

It is important to know that the people of Judah, were Exiled to Babylon in three Stages, and less returned than were taken there.

The Exile was predicted by Jeremiah (Jer 25.11-12)

The Book of Ezekiel (14-14 and 28-3), refer to Daniel as righteous and Famed for Wisdom.

The Book of Daniel is preserved in the 12 Chapter Masoretic text and in two longer Greek versions. The original Septuagint version, c 100BCE and the later Theodotion version from c, 2nd century CE. Both Greek texts contain three additions to Daniel.

The Prayer of Azariah and the song of the three holy children.

A Total of eight incomplete copies of the book of the Book of Daniel have been found at Qumran, two in Cave 1, five in cave 4, and one in cave 6.

None are complete, but between them they preserve text from eleven of Daniels 12 Chapters, and the twelfth is quoted in the Florilegium (a complete scroll) 4q174, showing that the book at Qumran did not lack this conclusion.

All eight manuscripts were copied between 125BCE (4QDane) and about 50CE (4QDanb) Showing that Daniel was being read at Qumran only 40 years after its composition.

All appear to preserve the 12 chapter Masoretic version rather than the longer Greek text.

All follow the bilingual nature of Daniel where the book opens in Hebrew, switches to Aramaic at 2.4b, then reverts to Hebrew at 8.1.

Biblical Timeline

The First Deportation was in 606BC.

The Top layer of Jewish Community.

The Royal Family, Court Officials and the temple Vessels.

This was to make sure the Jews did not Revolt.

Jehoiakim was left as a puppet king.

Daniel, Hananiah, Mishael, and Azariah were also exiled at this time.

The Babylonians renamed them as,

Belteshael, Shadrach, Meshack, and Abednego.

They were chosen to serve the Kings of Babylon.

They are of course the Heroes of the first part of the Book.

The Second Deportation was in 579BC.

These were the upper Class, Politicians, craftsmen.

Ezekiel was among these.

The Rest of the People were Exiled in 586BC.

When the City and the Temple was destroyed.

The First Return was in 538 BC,

When the Persians over threw Babylon,

Cyrus allowed about 50,000 to return under Zerubbabel.

The Second return was in 458 BC.

Under Ezra, when the rebuilding of the temple began.

The Third Group returned in 444 BC,

In fact a whole Jewish community remained in Iraq until the 1940s,

It is thought that The Wise men that followed the star came from this community, and were not the Gentiles that many teachers made them out to be.

The Book of Daniel Dovetails with the book of Esther

She lived in Susa the capital of the Medo-Persian Empire.

The Bible Predicts 735 Events, 27% of its verses focus on the Future.

593. 81% of these predictions have been fulfilled.

The Book of Daniel contains 166 Predictions, many are symbolic.

Chapter 11, An Amazing account of a series of events that took place centuries after Daniels lifetime.

There are 27 Specific Predictions in this chapter.

Which were fulfilled many years after Daniel Died.

The Book of Daniel is in two parts.

Part one Chapters 1-6 Is Mostly Miracles.

Part Two Chapters 7-12 is Mostly Prophecies.

The First Part is Easy to Understand,

The Second part are so difficult that often Adults rarely study it.

Daniel was Exiled in 605/606 BC.

When Babylon Conquered Judea.

Chaldea is another name for Babylon.

He was given the name of Belshazzar, a Babylonian God.

Diet

Daniel and his companions were being fed to look fat.

(For a Babylonian obesity was a sign of Prosperity).

They were all being fattened up for senior positions.

Daniel and his friends did not want to violate Gods dietary laws.

So they asked the man in charge of their training, if they could go on a Jewish diet for 10 days.

Then after the 10 days, to be compared with those on the Babylonian diet.

At the end of the 10 Days, they were found to be fitter than those on the Babylonian diet, so they were allowed to continue on the Jewish diet.

The Lesson here is, if you can stand your ground on small issues, then you can also on big issues.

In 606 BC Nebuchadnezzar had a Dream.

He wanted to know the meaning of his Dream, so he sent for his Wise Men.

The Problem was he had like most of us, had forgotten the description of the Dream, or maybe he was withholding the description, to test his wise men.

So his Wise men had to describe the Dream, and interpret it.

His Wise men were unable to do this, so he sent for Daniel.

Daniel said, your dream was a Giant Statue.

It had a head of Gold.

A body of Silver and Copper and legs of iron, Feet of Clay and Iron.

(This is where the saying *feet of clay* comes from).

The King said yes that's it.

The Interpretation of Daniel

Daniel said, The Golden Head is you King of your Empire.

The rest of the Body is the Unveiling of other Empires.

The Medes, the Persians, are the silver.

Followed by the Greeks (Alexandra the Great), (Copper).

Then the Romans. Strong as iron.

This metal fittingly represents the Roman Empire.

They had armies in iron armour, known as the iron legions of Rome.

The Romans would be followed by the feet of Iron and clay, an unstable mixture or Strength and Iron.

Think of the Armies that Followed the Romans

The King was very happy with Daniel, and made him his main adviser.

The Fiery Furnace

The King decided to have a Giant Statue Built.

90 feet high, 9 Feet wide.

He made a decree that Whenever the State Band played, everyone had to bow to the statue.

Shadrach, Meshach and Abednego refused to Bow. (Not sure where Daniel was at this time).

They were sentenced to be put in the Furnace.

The Furnace was heated 7 times hotter than normal.

It was so hot that the people who pushed the three men into the Furnace were burnt.

The King looked into the furnace and he could see 4 men in the Furnace.

Some speculate that this may had been the first appearance of the son of man.

Eventually the 3 men were let out of the Furnace unharmed.

The King Married a Beautiful young Princess from Persia

She came from Tehran which is the capital of Iran today.

The Princess was homesick, she missed the mountains, the animals and the flowers and trees where she came from.

The King heard her problem and promised to sort her problem out.

The King built a big Mountain.

He covered it with trees, scrubs and plants.

Today it is known as The Hanging gardens of Babylon (one of the wonders of the World).

On top of the Mountain, he put wild animals.

All this to please his wife.

One day he stood on the roof of his place and was struck by what he had achieved.

The King Said, Is this not Great Babylon, which I have built by my power and my Glory.

He Fell asleep and had a dream.

In the Dream he saw a Huge Tree that reached the sky.

Animals sheltered under its branches, Birds perched on other branches.

Then the Tree was cut down to just a stump and bound with iron.

But after a while it began to grow again.

The King asked Daniel to Interpret the Dream.

Daniel said that the King was the tree.

That he would be driven out of his Kingdom for 7 years.

He would crawl on the ground and eat grass, until He acknowledged that God was the Most High.

That God ruled the kingdoms of men and gave power to anyone he wanted to.

A year later God told the King that the Predictions would be fulfilled.

Sure enough the King went mad for 7 years.

His hair grew like feathers of an Eagle, His nails grew like Claws.

He ate grass. His people had to lock him in a Zoo.

At the End of the 7 Years He lifted his eyes to Heaven and said, God you are God.

God restored him to his throne, and made him greater than before.

Then the King made the Mistake of forcing all his people to worship God. Worship is an act of free will.

This is the story of the end of the Babylonian empire

The King had died, and was succeeded by his son Belshazzar.

He organised a big feast.

He had the Holy Vassals that had been brought from the Temple in Jerusalem, and used them at an orgy.

God is Always Watching

During the feast the King saw a finger start to write on a wall.

Mene, Mene, Tekel, Parsin.

The King was scared stiff.

He called for Daniel for an interpretation of the writing.

Daniel read, Your Reign is over, you did not measure up, and Your Kingdom is divided.

That very night the Persians attacked Babylon, the empire was finished and the King was killed.

This is of course the well known story of Daniel in the lion's den.

Things had moved on.

Daniel was now 90 years old.

There was a different king and empire.

Darius the Mede was king.

Anti-Semitism was rife.

The People of the Empire had to worship the king.

They were forbidden to pray to any other deity for a month.

Daniel had many enemies, people who were jealousy of him.

They knew that 3 times a day, he went to his upstairs front room and prayed towards Jerusalem.

They told Darius about this and they forced him to apply the penalty of disobedience.

Daniels was thrown to the lions.

The King did not want to do this.

He worried all night and rushed down to the den to check If Daniel had been eaten or not.

The Door was opened and Daniel walked out unharmed.

Daniel said that an Angel had shut the Lions mouths.

The King was happy to see Daniel Alive and had his accusers thrown into the lion's Den, with their wives and children.

Here we move from the Third person to the first person writing.

This section is primary for God's People.

This Section makes unique predictions that are so detailed, so dated in sequence and so accurate in the light of historical events, that it's simply history written down before it happened.

On the Negative side

They are not contiguous, not a series of events, following each other.

Neither in the correct order, neither do they start or finish at the same time.

On the Positive side

The Visions do vary in duration, some are brief, others covering a much longer period of time.

Some overlap each other, others are simultaneous.

They cover two periods of time.

The first period is leading up to the first coming of the Messiah.

The Second Period is leading up to the second Coming of Jesus.

In the First year of Belshazzar, Daniel had a dream of four beasts rising from the sea.

The Fourth a beast with ten horns, devours the whole Earth.

Treading it down and crushing it, and a further small horn appears and uproots three of the early horns.

The Ancient of Days Judges and destroys the beast, and one like the Son of man, is given everlasting kingship over the entire world.

A Divine being explains that the four beasts represent four kings, but that The Holy ones of the most high, would receive the everlasting Kingdom.

The fourth beast would be a fourth Kingdom with ten kings, and another king who would pull down the three kings and make war on the Holy ones for a time, two times and a half, after which the heavenly Judgement will be made against him and the Holy ones will receive the Everlasting Kingdom.

In the Third year of Belshazzar Daniel had a vision of a Ram and a Goat

The two beasts correspond to the parts of the giant Statue on Chapter 2.

The Ram had two mighty horns, one longer than the other, and it charges East and West and North, overpowering all other beasts.

A Goat with a single horn appears from the West and destroys the Ram.

The Goat becomes very powerful until the horn breaks off and is replaced with four lesser horns.

A small horn that grows very large, it stops the daily sacrifices and desecrates the sanctuary for two thousand three hundred evenings and mornings until the temple is cleansed.

The Angel Gabriel informs him that the ram represents the Medes and Persians, whose empire stretched from India, down to Egypt, down to Turkey.

Everything in this chapter came true.

The Goat Stands for the Greek Empire.

Alexandra the Great was given the nick name the Goat, because he was always charging ahead.

He was only 31 when he died, but he had conquered the whole civilised world.

He was revered as one of histories greatest conquers.

He was a self-indulgent man, and his sinful life style contributed to his downfall.

When he died his Empire was divided between his 4 generals.

Lysinicus was given Turkey, Cassander and Greece.

Ptolemy had Egypt, Seleucid and Syria.

So Israel was trapped between Lysinicus and Ptolemy, leaving Israel facing difficulty as a result.

In the first year of Darius the Mede, Daniel Meditates on the word of Jeremiah that the desolation of Jerusalem would last seventy years, he confesses the sin of Israel and pleads for God to restore Israel and the desolated sanctuary of the temple.

The Angel Gabriel explains that the seventy years stand for seventy "weeks "of years(490 years), during which the temple will first be destroyed, then later defiled by a " Prince who is to come" Until the decree end is poured out.

This Chapter contains a prediction of how long it will be before the new king arrives.

Bible Scholars call this passage Daniels Seventy Weeks, and much ink has been spent on conjecture about its meaning, but theories abound.

Daniel is told that seventy sevens are decreed for Israel, but it is important to realise that the word seven means not a week but seven years.

So it isn't Seventy weeks.

At all but seventy sevens, that's 490 Years.

So from the time of the decree to go back from Babylon to Jerusalem until the coming of the king would be 483 years. (IE 69 Sevens).

It is not clear what decree Daniel is referring to, nor if he is using the Babylonian Calendar based on the solar year of 365 and a quarter days, or the Jewish calendar of 360 days.

There were 4 Decrees

The Decree of Cyrus began the return of the Exiles in 536BC.

The Decree of Darius allowed more people to return to Jerusalem

There were two Decrees by Artaxerxes which enabled Nehemiah to return and rebuild the Temple.

Whatever Decree you choose to count from The Allotted years end at either the Birth or Baptism of Jesus.

Either way 500 years later Jesus was born.

So Daniel predicted the coming of Jesus 500 years before it happened.

Daniel was also told it would be a long time until the end of the Sixty-ninth Seven, when the king will come, but crucially, he left the seventieth week out of these events.

Maybe that in the seventieth week he was looking right past the first coming, to the second coming.

There was a huge gap in time between the sixty – ninth and the seventieth seven.

So this week equals a seven year period that has not taken place.

When the Antichrist will appear.

According to the text, a pact will be forced and a treaty with Israel will be under threat, during this time persecution will be especially fierce.

Sacrifices will cease and the temple will be desecrated in the same manner as at the time of Antiochus Epiphanes, which implies that it must have been rebuilt at some time.

In the third year of Cyrus, Daniel sees in a vision an Angel who explains that he is in the midst of a war with the prince of Persia assisted only by Michael, the prince of Greece will shortly come, but first He will reveal what will happen to Daniels people.

This covers a further revelation which causes Daniel great consternation.

It shows that all earthly conflicts are matched by a heavenly conflict between Angels and demonic forces.

The Chapter tells us that behind every earthly power and every growing kingdom, there is a demonic prince.

There is demonic influence behind people who want to take over or devastate other countries.

This chapter mentions the prince of Persia and the prince of Greece.

God sends Michael to overcome them.

Some Christians believe that before they launch an evangelistic campaign, they must first identify the evil demon over the city or town and bind him before they start.

Jesus did not say "go into all the world, find the demons and bind them", but go and make disciples of all the nations.

We should leave spiritual warfare to the Angels, unless demons make themselves manifest.

A future king of Persia will make war on the king of Greece, a "mighty king" will arise and wield power until his empire is broken up and given to others, and finally the king of the south (verse 8 Egypt) will go to war with the "king of the north".

After many battles a contemptible person will become king of the north.

This king will invade the south two times, the first time with success, but on his second he will be stopped by "ships of Kittim".

(According to Daniel, the only government on earth powerful enough to soundly defeat the Rebel and his associates in battle is an island nation far to the west across the sea called Kitten.

Associated with Javan (The Western Empire responsible for the defeating the ram)

Kittim appears destined in prophecy to rise up out of the collapse of Javan

To become the last surviving remnant of western civilization at the close of history.

With the discovery of the new world a few hundred years ago, the boundaries of western civilization were greatly expanded, Kittim (or West) of Daniels time was Rome.

The Ships of the West that opposed the evil Antiochus — the beast of Jerusalem – where Roman ships, and the "islands of the sea" in his day were the islands of the Mediterranean.

But Daniels Prophesies were not about Antiochus of his times, they were about our time and the future, and in our days, the boundaries of the west have been moved across the Atlantic Ocean to include the United States.

Because the world is larger today it is almost certain that the provinces occupied and fought over by the beast will involve greater boundaries than the place names listed in Daniels Prophesy, for this reason , Daniels place names must be seen as Symbolic representations of future boundaries that mirror them in the last days.

For this reason, the islands of the sea (Dn. 11: 18, 1s, 24:15, Ez, 26:18) must be considered in terms of the American continent.

What Daniels words seem to imply, therefore, is that although the beast will be given power over Rome, he will not have power over the military might of America.

At least not until the very end, because the prophecies indicate that the rebels final attack on this last western power will have terminal consequences for world history (Dn 11:44-12:1).

The Power of this West (Kittim) in Daniels Prophecies is very significant.

When the two northern kings destined to head the ten-nation

Eastern confederation of the last days appears, neither of them will be successful in their efforts to vanquish this western force in their struggle to take world control.

On the contrary, according to Daniel, every time the two engage in military combat, the west will emerge victorious.

Antiochus 1V Epiphanes, the Ruler on whom a great many of Daniels Prophecies are thought to be based, had to measure every one of his moves because of the superior strength of the Romans in the west who were displeased with his aggressions, and, on several occasions, blocked his moves and defeated him on the battlefields.

After being warned by the Romans to pull back, Antiochus was overwhelmingly defeated by them because he ignored their threats. (Dn, 11:30).

Angered by this bitter defeat at the hands of the Romans.

Antiochus turned his wrath inwards-towards the Holy Covenant and the people who adhered to it.).

The Most astonishing prediction in the whole Bible

In 35 Verses 135 Major events are predicted, covering a total of 366 years.

Some Scholars say Daniel could not have written this.

It must have been written later.

But God knows the beginning and the end, and he enabled Daniel to write his book.

There is a mention of Antiochus 1V Epiphanes.

He became the Scourge of the Jews.

He became Regent of the Greek State of Seleucid, just north of Israel, and he was the Guardian of the young boy king.

But he killed the Boy and made himself King.

He was a terrible tyrant and was determined to wipe out the Jewish religion.

He desecrated the temple by sacrificing a pig on the altar

He Filled the Altar Rooms with Prostitutes.

He even erected an image of Jupiter in the Temple.

He will turn back to his own country, and on his way his soldiers will desecrate the temple, abolish the daily sacrifice, and set up abomination of desolation.

He will defeat and subjugate Libya and Egypt, but" reports from the east and north will alarm him" and he will meet his end" between the sea and the Holy Mountain".

Antiochus 1V Epiphanes   Was the eight in a succession of 26 kings who ruled from 175-164 BC, over the Syrian section of Alexandra's Empire.

It was the Seleucid Empire. A Hellenistic State.

He was referred to by Daniel as the little Horn in Daniel 8:9.

Antiochus Massacred 40,000 Jews, selling an equal number into slavery.

It was so dreadful that the Jews could not stand it, and the result was the Maccabean Revolt.

Judean rebels became known as the Maccabees.

They fought the Seleucid Empire from 167-160 BC.

They were outnumbered by the Seleucid Arm but fought a Guerrilla war.

Eventually the Maccabees won.

Antiochus is, in a sense, the parallel of the Antichrist at the end of history.

The Division between Chapters 11 and 12 is unhelpful since 12 continues to focus on the antichrist, and is concerned with events associated with the second coming of Christ including the resurrection of both Good and Bad people.

The King has come once, he has not yet taken over the world.

For that we wait his return.

At this Time Michael will come.

It will be a time of Great Distress, but all those whose names are written will be delivered.

Multitudes who sleep in the dust of the earth will awake, some to everlasting life, others to shame and everlasting contempt, those who are wise will shine like the brightness of the heavens, and those who lead many to righteousness, like the stars for ever and ever.

In the final verses the remaining time to the end is revealed, a time, times and half a time (three years and a half).

Daniel fails to understand and asks again what will happen, and is told "from the time that the daily sacrifice is abolished and the abomination that causes desolation is set up, there will be 1,290 days.

Blessed is the one who waits for and reaches the end of the 1,335 days.

Predictions not yet fulfilled

Jesus has come once, but has not yet taken over the kingdoms of the World. For that we await his Return.

The Visions

The Lion with Wings - Maybe this is America and the UK

The Bear – is this Russia?

The Leopard with wings and 4 heads – maybe The Arab World?

The Kingdom is Clearly Gods Kingdom.

Macarthur's commentary

Macarthur says that the lion is Babylon, the Bear is The Medo – Persian Empire, and The Leopard is Greece, the fourth beast (No such animal exists) is Rome.

Personally I believe the first version by David Pawson (author of *Unlocking the Bible*). The Rest I am not sure.

It's Evident that What Happens in Chapter 12, is to come.

Daniel was often unaware of the meaning of what he was seeing. So it's clear that's it's not for Daniel sake but for later Generations.

There will soon be a period of 400 years with no Prophets.

So the Book of Daniel was to partly aid the people of God during this period. Nothing was recorded about Daniel after the completion of his book.

Ezekiel

By the time of Ezekiel, all that remained of Judah was the city of Jerusalem, now under foreign domination.

Finally the Babylonians returned and besieged the city for two and a half years. Then the exile started.

Zedekiah was the last puppet king of Judah.

Ezekiel, was the author of the book Ezekiel.

He was the son of Buzzi, born into a priesthood (Kohen) lineage of the patrilineal line of Ithamar, and resident of Anathoth.

He gives a chronology for the first divine encounter which he will present. He states that it happened "in the thirtieth year," which may be a reference to his age at the time. In such a case, the approximate year of birth is 622 BC. He also dates the event 5 years after the exile of King of Judah Jehoiachin by the Babylonians, a recurring dating pattern through the book. Josephus claims that at the request of Nebuchadnezzar 11, Babylonian armies exiled three thousand Jews from Judah, after deposing King Jehoiahin in 598 BC. Some argue that the book of Ezekiel was written by the great Assembly because a prophet was not allowed to write down prophecies while being outside Israel.

Living in Babylon

Ezekiel and his wife lived on the bank of the Chebar River, in Tel Abib, where exiles from Judah came to seek his prophetic insights.

Ezekiel's wife died rather young, in the ninth year of exile, when he was 34 years of age.

Prophetic career

Ezekiel describes his calling to be a prophet by going into great detail about his encounter with God and four living creatures of Cherubim with four wheels that stayed beside the creatures. For the next five years he incessantly prophesied and acted out the destruction of Jerusalem and its temple, which was met with some opposition. However, Ezekiel and his contemporaries like Jeremiah, another prophet who was living in Jerusalem at the time, witnessed the fulfilment of their prophecies when Jerusalem was finally sacked by the Babylonians. Ezekiel was 50 years old when he began to have visions of a new Temple. He served as a prophet for at least 22 years. Ezekiel last experienced an encounter with God in April 570 BC. His time of death has not been recorded.

Some of his predictions are remarkably detailed. Let's take one. Here Ezekiel predicts the downfall of the fishing port of Tyre. Ezekiel predicts that one day Tyre will be razed to the ground, the whole city would be thrown into the sea.

This came true, when Alexander the Great approached Tyre on his way up from Egypt with a great army.

The people of Tyre realising he did not have a navy, they simply got into their boats and rowed to an island half a mile from shore.

When Alexander saw a lot of people standing on this island, he commanded that every brick, stone or plank of timber be thrown into the sea to build a causeway to the island. When it was completed his army crossed and defeated the people of Tyre.

According to the Midrash CANTICLES RABBAH, it was Ezekiel whom the three pious men, Hananiah, Mishael, and Azariah (also called Shadrach, Messhach, and Abednego in the Bible) asked for advice as to whether they should resist Nebuchadnezzar's command and choose death by fire rather than worship his idol. At first God revealed to the prophet that they could not hope for a miraculous rescue; whereupon the prophet was greatly grieved, since these three men constituted the "remnant of Judah", But after they had left the house of the prophet, fully determined to sacrifice their lives to God, Ezekiel received this revelation: "thou dost believe indeed that I will abandon them. That shall not happen; but do thou let them carry out their intention according to their pious dictates, and tell them nothing."

Mordecai

Mordecai is one the main personalities in the book of Esther. He was the son of Jair, of the tribe of Benjamin.

Mordecai's genealogy in the second chapter of the book of Esther is given as a descendant of Kish of the tribe of Benjamin. Kish was also the name of the father of King Saul, and the Talmud accords Mordecai the status of descendant of the first King of Israel.

The Talmud lists Mordecai and Esther as prophets. The Talmud says that Mordecai prophesied in the second year of Darius.

Biblical account

Mordecai resided in Susa, the metropolis of Persia (now Iran). He adopted his orphaned cousin (Esther 2:7), Hadassah (Esther), whom he brought up as if she was his own daughter. When "young Virgins" were sought, she was taken into the presence of King Xerxes and was made Queen in the place of the exiled Queen Vashti.

Mordecai was referred to subsequently as one of those who "sat in the Kings gate" to indicate his position of closeness to the King. While holding this office, he discovered a plot of the king's chamberlain Bigthan and Teresh to assassinate the King. Because of Mordecai's vigilance, the plot was foiled. His services to the king in this matter were duly recorded in the King's royal diary.

Haman the Agagite had been raised to the highest position at court. In spite of the King's decree that all should prostate themselves before Haman, Mordecai refused to do so. Though the Hebrew Scriptures attest to Israelites or Jews bowing out of respect and submission (Gen 33:3, 2 Sam24:8), Haman was a descendant of the Amalekites, their ancient enemies (Esther 3:1; 1 Sam 15:8). Haman, stung by Mordecai's refusal, resolved to accomplish his death in a wholesale murder of the Jewish exiles throughout the Persian Empire. Learning of Harman's scheme, Mordecai communicated with Queen Esther regarding it, and by her bold intervention the scheme was frustrated by distributing arms to the Jews of Susa and other Persian cities where there lived and clashed with Haman's Militia, until the King rescinded the edict to murder the empire's Jews. Mordecai was raised to a high rank, donned in the royal grey cloak, and Haman was executed on gallows he had by anticipation erected for Mordecai.

Seraiah

Seraiah, is the name of several people in the Bible.

- 1/ the Father of Joab (1 Chronicles 4:13, 14).
- 2/ the Grandfather of Jehu (1 Chronicles 4: 35)
- 3/ Seraiah the son of Tanhumeth (Jer 40:8)
- 4/ the Ruler of the Temple (Neh 11:11)

❖ 5/ Seraiah ben Neriah. The son of Neriah. When Zedekiah made a journey to Babylon to do homage to Nebuchadnezzar, Seraiah had charge of the royal gifts to be presented on that occasion.

Jeremaiah took advantage of the occasion, and sent with Seraiah a word of cheer to the exiles in Babylon, and an announcement of the doom in store for that guilty city. The roll containing this message (Jeremaiah 50:1-8) Seraiah was to read to the exiles, and then, after fixing a stone to it, he was to throw it into the Euphrates, uttering, as it sank, the prayer recorded in Jer. 51 : 59-64.

Babylon was at this time in the height of its glory, the greatest and most powerful monarchy in the world. Scarcely seventy years elapsed when the words of the prophet were all fulfilled. Jer 51:59.

Now Seraiah was Chief Chamberlain,

Chapter Seven - Prophets of the Return: Ezra to Zechariah

Ezra

Ezra (480-440 BC), was a Jewish scribe and priest. According to the Hebrew Bible he was a descendant of Seraiah (Ezra 7:1) the last high priest to serve in the first Temple (Kings 2 25:18), and a close relative of Joshua the first high priest of the second Temple (Chronicles 1 5:40-41). He returned from Babylonian Exile and reintroduced the Torah in Jerusalem (Ezra 7-10). According to Ieadras, a Greek translation of the book of Ezra still in use in Eastern Orthodoxy.

The Book of Ezra describes how he led a group of Judean exiles living in Babylon to their home city of Jerusalem (Ezra 8: 2-14) where he is said to have enforced observance of the Torah.

A few parts of the book of Ezra are written in Aramaic, and the majority in Hebrew, Ezra himself being skilled in both languages. Ezra was living in Babylon when in the seventh year (457 BC) of Artaxerxes, king of Persia, the king sent him to Jerusalem to teach the laws of God to any who did not know them. Ezra led a large body of exiles back to Jerusalem, where he discovered that Jewish men had been marrying non-Jewish women. He tore his garments in despair and confessed the sins of Israel before God, then braved the opposition of his own countrymen to purify the community by enforcing the dissolution of the sinful marriages. Some years later Artaxerxes sent Nehemiah to Jerusalem as governor with the task of rebuilding the City walls. Once this task was completed Nehemiah had Ezra read the Law of Moses (The Torah) to the assembled Israelites, and the people and priests entered into a covenant to keep the law and separate themselves from all other peoples.

The fourth book of Ezra, was written AD 100, probably in Hebrew-Aramaic. It was one of the most important sources for Jewish theology at the end of the 1st century. In this book, Ezra has a seven part prophetic revelation, converses with an angel of God three times and has four visions. Ezra, thirty years into the Babylonian exile (4 Ezra 3:1/2), recounts the siege of Jerusalem and the destruction of Solomon's Temple. This would place these revelations in the year 557 BC, a full century before the date given in the canonical Ezra.

God's justice in the face of the triumph of the heathens over the pious, the course of World history in terms of teaching of the four Kingdoms, the function of the law, the eschatological judgement, the appearance on Earth of the heavenly Jerusalem, the Messianic Period, at the end of which the Messiah will die, the end of the world and the coming of the next, and the last judgement. Ezra restores the law that was destroyed with the burning of the temple in Jerusalem.

He dictated 24 books for the public and another 70 for the wise alone.

At the end, he was taken up to Heaven like Enoch and Elijah.

Haggai

The first thing they wanted to build when they returned to Jerusalem was a temple, but the task was daunting, they faced opposition from the Samaritans and when Darius replaced Cyrus, they lost the subsidy that Cyrus had given to rebuild the temple.

They stopped building after two years, and for fourteen years didn't put another stone on the temple.

Building a temple was a luxury they could not afford, food was becoming short and expensive.

Eventually the people asked "why"? And begun to discuss what was going wrong.

It was into this depressing situation that Haggai spoke.

The People failed to realize that God had made things go wrong. Haggai said their problems were because they had stopped building the temple.

The people responded positively, and returned to the task.

The best welfare state ever is the Kingdom of Heaven, Jesus said "if you put God first, all these other things will look after themselves.

Haggai spoke about the people needing to become clean. Dirty people will make clean things dirty. So before we do anything in God's name we need to cleanse ourselves first.

(This doesn't mean having a bath)

Haggai, was a Hebrew prophet during the building of the second temple in Jerusalem, and one of the twelve Minor Prophets. Also he was the author of the Book of Haggai.

He was the first of the three post-exile prophets from the Neo-Babylonian Exile of the house of Judah, (with Zechariah and Malachi).

After these God didn't send further Revelation for over 400 years.

For 400 years the Jews had to tell their children, "someday God will speak to us again" it was not until John the Baptist came that his voice was heard again.

Very little is known of his personal history. He may have been one of the captives taken to Babylon by Nebuchadnezzar.

He began his ministry about sixteen years after the return of the Jews to Judah (520BC). The work of rebuilding the temple had been put to a stop through the intrigues of the Samaritans.

After having been suspended for fourteen years, the work was resumed through the efforts of Haggai and Zechariah. They exhorted the people, which roused them from their lethargy.

(Cyrus conquered Babylon in 538BC. He told all exiles that they could return home, provided that they built a temple in which they would pray to their God on his behalf.

Only 50,000 Jews returned.

Most had established themselves as merchants and had become quiet wealthy. Jerusalem did not have the same advantages and seemed a bleak prospect.

Imagine this, you have a nice brick house, and a good job. Then you are offered the chance to move to a town which was in ruins. You have little food, you sleep in tents maybe. Your job won't be to make money as you had been doing, but to build a church.)

Considering the hardship, maybe 50,000 is a good number.

Malachi

The background of the Book of Malachi is similar to Haggai and Zechariah.

It was written 100 years after the return of Judah from exile in Babylon.

Things were not good, Jerusalem was still relatively deserted. Recent harvests had been poor, lack of food made life hard.

The Temple had been completed in 520 BC, but it was so small compared to Solomon's Temple, that it had done little to lift moral.

Although Nehemiah had repaired the walls, the people preferred to live in the country where they could hide if they were attacked.

The good news was that the people had learned their lesson about idolatry in exile.

Malachi, writer of the Book of Malachi, the last book of the Neviim (prophets) section in the Hebrew Bible. He delivered his prophesies about 420 BC, after the second return of Nehemiah (Neh 13:6), or possibly before his return. Never again did they go after other God's.

But the people were attending the Temple out of tradition, a ritual without reality.

There is more of God's speech in Malachi, than in any other of the prophetic books.

Opinions vary as to the prophets exact date, but nearly all scholars agree that Malachi prophesied during the Persian period, and after the reconstruction and dedication of the second temple in 516 BC (Malachi 1:10).

Nehemiah
Nehemiah, was a happy man and encouraged others to be the same.

He was a Man of prayer, others like Ezra were bible men.

He was an emotional man, at times showing deep sorry, other times great happiness. Also he was a social man and a natural leader.

Nehemiah, was the central figure of the book of Nehemiah, which describes his work in rebuilding Jerusalem during the second Temple period. He was Governor of Persian Judea under Artaxerxes 1 of Persia (5th century BC).

In the 20th year of Artaxerxes, King of Persia, (445/444BC). Nehemiah was cup bearer to the King. Learning that the remnant in Judah were in destress and that the walls of Jerusalem were broken down, he asked the King for permission to return and rebuild the city.

Artaxerxes sent him to Judah as governor of the province with a mission to rebuild, letters explaining his support for the venture, and provisions for timber from the Kings forest. Once there, Nehemiah defied the opposition of Judah's enemies on all sides- Samaritans, Ammonites, Arabs and Philistines-and rebuilt the walls within 52 days, from the Sheep gate in the north, the Hananel Tower at the north west corner, the First gate in the west, the Furnaces Tower at the Temple Mount's south west corner, the Dung gate in the south, and the gate beneath the Golden gate in the east.

He then took measures to repopulate the city and purify the Jewish Community, enforcing the cancellation of debt, assisting Ezra to promulgate the Law of Moses, and enforcing the divorce of Jewish men from their non-Jewish wives.

After 12 years as governor, during which he ruled with justice and righteousness, he returned to the King of Persia. After some time he

Returned to Jerusalem, only to find the people had fallen back into their evil ways. Non-Jews were permitted to conduct business inside Jerusalem, on the Sabbath and to keep rooms in the Temple. Greatly Angered (I think this was an understatement), he purified the Temple and the priests and Levites and enforced the observance of the laws of Moses.

(I presume he had brought Persian soldiers with him as support).

Do these Israelites ever learn? But look at ourselves, do we ever stop Sinning?

Zechariah

Zechariah, prophesied for two years, his prophesising overlapped Haggai. Both there prophesies were very similar, with Zechariah carrying on where Haggai left off. He was a priest as well as a prophet.

His call was about October/November 520 BC

He prophesied that one day the Priests will take over from Kings and Prophets as leaders of the Nation. By the time Jesus came, there were only Priests.

Zechariah, was the eleventh of the twelve Minor Prophets.

He was a prophet of Judah.

According to Ezra 5:1 and Ezra 6: 14 Iddo was the father of Zechariah, according to Zechariah 1:1 Barachiah was his father and Iddo was his grandfather.

In the gospel of Matthew, Jesus said that Zechariah son of Barachiah, was killed between the altar and the sanctuary.

Conclusion

We are now nearing the end of the Old Testament.

We started with God making everything including man.

He looked down and was happy.

Then man went wrong and did evil things.

Eventually God got so angry that he caused a flood to destroy everything apart from a few good people and some animals to start again.

Let's look at the Patriots

These were prophets. The Jews continued to sin, then repent with God forgiving them.

Eventually Jacob and his family settled in Egypt and everything was good. Then years later the Jews had become slaves to the Egyptians.

Moses was chosen to lead the Jews out of Egypt, with the offer of the Promised Land.

This was a long Journey where the Israelites went back and forth from worshiping Idols to worshiping God.

Time and Again they were punished, But the seemed unable to fully understand the lesson, that God will not accept his people worshiping any other God.

Prophets had to keep being sent to warn the Israelites of their sins.

Despite all this God still loved them (as he loves us, even when we fall)

(I don't know about you, but by now I would have given up on the Jews).

The Bible says that God is our father.

Think about being the parent of a child.

You look down on your baby and fall in love with it.

Sometimes your baby/child makes you happy but at other times they are naughty and make you angry.

When they are naughty you have to punish them, but you hope they will learn not to do wrong and grow into a responsible adult.

As the Old Testament gets to its end, God is still wondering what to do with his children the Israelites.

Let's look at God

The Trinity - God the father, Jesus the son and the Holy Spirit. They are all part of the Deity.

How can three be one you may ask?

One explanation I was once given is this.

If we see God the father as water, Jesus the son as ice, and the Holy Spirit as steam. All three are water in various forms.

The same as God the Father, Jesus the son and the Holy Spirit are all God.

So when God came up with the solution to conquer sin, so we could all go to Heaven.

He sent his son Jesus as the sacrifice for our sin.

God was in fact sending himself to pay the price of our sin.

So God so loved us that he died for us.

He took all the sins we had ever committed on his shoulders, so we that believe could be with him in Heaven.

Amen

PART TWO - THE NEW TESTAMENT

The Old Testament covered about 2,000 years, followed by a 400 year gap between the old and New Testament, When God was silent.

In the following section, we will look at the Book of Acts, The Life of St Paul, and learn about the 12 disciples.

The Disciples were ordinary people like you and me.

They were going about their work.

Some were fishing, others collected Tax's etc.

They had families, some were Married.

But when Jesus called them, they left everything and followed him.

We will read what was before these men.

Hunger, persecution, and for eleven of the twelve a painful death.

Some people say that Jesus was only a man, but to get the disciples to leave their homes and follow him to an unknown destiny.

Jesus was far more than a Man, he must be the son of God.

We will start with a look at the 12 disciples.

The Twelve Disciples

The Twelve disciples/Apostles of Jesus were to become the foundation stones of his Church.

Many of the Books in the New Testament were written by Disciples.

We will study what discipleship meant in the time of Jesus.

Jesus called twelve men to be his Disciples.

> *Peter*
>
> *James*
>
> *John*
>
> *Andrew*
>
> *Bartholomew or Nathanael*
>
> *James, the lesser or Younger*
>
> *Judas*
>
> *Jude or Thaddeus*
>
> *Matthew or Levi*
>
> *Philip*
>
> *Simon the Zealot*
>
> *Thomas.*

Peter

We will start with Peter, normally excepted as the spokesperson of the Disciples.

In my research I found so much about Peter that I could have written a book just about just him.

Peter became one of the boldest witnesses for the life a death of Jesus.

His beginnings were humble.

He was born about 1 BC, and died around 67 AD.

Peter was originally named Simon. Jesus changed his name to Peter.

The name Peter means Rock.

He was a Galilean fishermen and was the brother of Andrew.

The brothers came from the village of Bethsaida (John 1: 43, 12-21)

Peter was married. He was also a follower of John the Baptist.

Fishermen in the time of Jesus were gruff, unkempt, vile, scruffy, and often used vulgar language.

They were full of vigour and had boisterous tempers.

Maybe this is why James and John were called the sons of thunder (Mark 3:17).

Fishing was a hard life, the storms came quickly upon the Sea of Galilee and were fierce and furious. The storms could easily sink the 20-30 foot boats they used.

Peter was always putting his foot in his mouth, but when Jesus told Peter and his brother Andrew to follow him. They left everything without a second thought.

They left behind their Boats, Nets, their business, and their families.

Then followed Jesus with just the clothes they wore.

Would you just drop everything and follow Jesus? Bearing in mind they had only met him a little while ago.

Mark or Peter?

There is extremely reliable evidence through Church tradition and early Church Historians that the **Gospel of Mark** is really the Gospel of Peter.

It is believed that John Mark (who you will read about in the Book of Acts), Wrote the Gospel of Mark.

John Mark was not a disciple and he was not an Apostle.

There is little doubt Mark had written the story of Peter. Dictated to him by Peter. Many intimate details were described in Mark. Some of the events included Peter, John, and James who were often alone with Jesus, like the Transfiguration, are like a first-person retelling of the story.

When you get to reading the Gospel of Mark, see if you can more clearly come to the realization that this had to be Peter's eyewitness account- an account that only Peter could tell.

The Rock

One day Jesus was talking with the disciples. (Matthew 16: 13-19).

Jesus asks "Who do people say that the son of man is?" The Disciples give various answers. Then he asks, "Who do you say that I am?" Simon Peter answers, "You are the messiah, the son of the living God." Jesus then declares:

Blessed are you son of Jonah, for this was not revealed to you by flesh or blood, but by my father in Heaven. And I tell you are Cephas (Peter) (Petros), and on this rock (Petra) I will build my church, and the gates of hades will not overcome it. I will give you the keys of the Kingdom of Heaven; whatever you bind on earth will be bound in Heaven, and whatever you loose on earth will be loosed in Heaven.

The Last Supper

At the beginning of the last supper, Jesus washed his disciples' feet.

Peter refused to let Jesus wash his feet, but when Jesus responded: "if I don't wash your feet, you have no part with me". Peter replied:

"Lord, not my feet only, but also my hands and my head".

During the last supper, Jesus foretold that Peter would deny him three times, before the Cockcrow.

This Peter did without realising.

When the Roman Soldiers arrived, Peter using a sword to cut an ear off a servant of the high priest named Malchus.

Jesus touched the ear and miraculously healed it.

In the Gospel of Luke is a record of Jesus telling Peter; "Simon, Simon, behold, Satan hath desired to have you that he may sift you as wheat; but I have prayed for you, that you fail not; and when you are converted, strengthen your Brothers.

Resurrection

In John's Gospel, Peter is the first person to enter the empty tomb, although the women and the beloved disciple see it before him.

The women report of the empty tomb, but Peter is the only one to enter the tomb.

The Early Church

Peter was a very important person within the early Church.

He delivered a significant open – air sermon during Pentecost.

Peter took the lead in selecting a replacement for Judas Iscariot.

He was twice arraigned, with John, before the Sanhedrin and directly defied them. He went on a missionary journey to Lydda, Joppa and Caesarea, becoming instrumental in the decision to evangelise the Gentiles.

About Halfway through, the Book of Acts, the attention turns away from Peter to the activities of Paul, the Bible is mostly silent on what happened to Peter afterwards.

Rome

When Peter arrived in Rome, there were already many Christians.

Peter preached the word of God publically in Rome.

Peter arrived in Rome during the reign of Nero.

(Not a good time for Christians, Nero eventually blamed the Christians for the Fire that destroyed a part of Rome. He then persecuted them).

Through the power of God committed unto him, he performed miracles, and, by turned many to Christ.

It is believed that Peter the humble fisherman became the first Bishop of Rome.

In the days leading up to Peter's death, almost all of the apostles had been martyred.

From an arrogant, cocky, man of thunder, he became a humble, willing, obedient servant of the Lord even to death, knowing that he would be reunited with his beloved Saviour. He was 65 years old, of which his last 33 would be devoted to proclaiming the Gospel of Jesus Christ.

In the reign of Nero he was sentenced to be crucified. Peter said "he was not worthy to be crucified as Jesus was" so he was crucified upside down, with his head facing the earth.

Peter came from a lowly beginning, and ended up as the first Pope.

Andrew

Andrew was the brother of Peter, both sons of John.

He was originally a disciple of John the Baptist.

John the Baptist was standing with two of his disciples; and he looked at Jesus as he walked, and said "behold, the Lamb of God!" the two disciples heard him say this, and they followed Jesus.

Jesus turned, and saw them following, and said to them, "what do you seek? " (This is interesting as I would had said "what do you want") and they said "Rabbi" (teacher), "where are you staying?" He said to them, "Come and see." They came and saw where he was staying: and they stayed with him that day.

One of the two who followed Jesus was Andrew.

He rushed home and Told his brother Simon (Peter), and told him" We have found the Messiah" (Which means Christ).

He then took Simon to meet Jesus. Jesus looked at Simon, and said, "So you are Simon the son of John? You shall be called Peter.

The next day Jesus decided to go to Galilee. And he found Philip and said to him, "Follow me." Phillip was from Bethsaida, the same city that Andrew and Peter came from.

Andrew was one of the first to follow Jesus because he has an enquiring mind, and he was looking for the truth.

Andrew was one of the inner circle of the Disciples, He with Peter, James and John were on the Mount of Olives with Jesus when he spoke about the coming Cataclysm in Jerusalem.

Andrew introduced others to Jesus. Although circumstances placed him in a position where it would have been easy for him to become jealous and resentful, he was optimistic and content in second place. His main purpose in life was to bring others to Jesus.

Andrew preached in Scythia, also along the Black sea and the river Dnieper as far as Kiev, and then to Novgorod. He founded the See of Byzantium (to be known as Constantinople and Istanbul) in AD 38.

He also preached in Thrace, and Achaea.

For a man on foot or Donkey, he travelled a long way spreading the Message of Jesus.

It was in Achaia (Greece), in the town of Patra that he died a Martyr.

Andrew healed Governor Aepeas' wife and she then became a Christian. Shortly after the Governors' brother became a Christian.

Aepeas flew into a temper. He had Andrew arrested and condemned to be crucified.

Andrew felt unworthy to be crucified as Jesus. (This is strange as Peter also felt like this, ending up being crucified upside down.)

So, he was crucified on an X shaped cross. This is now called the St Andrew cross.

James the Elder

James, the Elder, was the son of Zebedee and Salome, and the Brother of John the Apostle.

He was a fisherman as were Peter and Andrew.

He lived in Bethsaida, Capernaum and Jerusalem.

He preached in Jerusalem and throughout Judea.

As you can see he didn't travel as far as other disciples.

He was beheaded under the orders of Herod, AD 44 (Acts 12: 1, 2).

He was a member of the inner circle, who were given special privileges.

There is little about James in the Bible. His name never appears apart from when with his brother, John.

The brothers were always together (Mark 1: 19-20; Matthew 4:21; Luke 5: 1-11).

James was a man of courage and forgiveness, a man without jealousy, who lived in the shadow of his brother John, a man of great faith.

He was the first of the disciples to be martyred.

John the Apostle

John was born around AD 6, and was the son of Zebedee and Salome and brother of James, also one of the twelve disciples.

John, like his brother James lived in Bethsaida, Capernaum and Jerusalem. He was also a fisherman.

John wrote The Gospel of John, 1 John, 11 John, 111 John, and Revelations.

He was a man of action, also very ambitious; and a man with an explosive temper and an intolerant heart.

John and his brother James, came from a more wealthy family than the rest of the disciples. As their father hired servants to help in their fishing business (Mark 1:20) maybe John felt above the other disciples.

John was a close friend of Peter. They often acted together, but Peter, however, was the spokesman for the disciples.

Let's have a quick look at John.

A Man of Action; that sounds good and useful.

Ambitious, an explosive temper, an intolerant heart.

Wow I am not sure I would had chosen John.

But Jesus called him his beloved disciple.

In time John mellowed. In the later part of his life, he had forgotten everything, including his ambition and explosive temper, all except his Lords command of Love.

Patmos

John was banished to Patmos during the persecutions under Emperor Domitian. Revelation 1:9 says that the author wrote the book on Patmos.

An attempt was made on John's life at Patmos, by giving him a chalice of poison but God spared him.

All the other disciples had died or had been martyred at the time of John's death.

John died of natural causes at the age of about 93/94 in AD 100.

Bartholomew

Bartholomew was the son of Talmia. He lived in Cana of Galilee. He was the only discliple who came from royal blood, or had a noble birth. His name means son of Talmai (2 Samuel 3: 3).

Talmia was king of Geshur whose daughter, Maacah, was the wife of David, mother of Absolom.

Bartholomew was not his first name, this was probable Nathanael, who Jesus called "an Israelite indeed, in whom there is no guile" (John 1:47).

There is little information about him in the Bible.

He was a great searcher of the scripture and a scholar in the law and the prophets. He became a man who completely surrendered to Jesus.

Of the many miracles he performed before and after his death, two are known to the people in a small island of Lipari.

The tradition of the people was to take the solid silver and gold statue of Bartholomew, from inside the Cathedral of St Bartholomew and carry it down to the town. On one occasion, while carrying the statue down the hill to the town, it suddenly became very heavy and had to be set down. When the men carrying the statue regained their strength, they lifted it again for a second time. After a few seconds, it got even heavier. They set it down again, then attempted once more to pick it up. They managed to lift it but had to put it down one last time.

Within seconds, Walls further downhill collapsed. If the statue had been able to be lifted, all the towns' people would had been killed.

During World War two, the Fascist regime looked for ways to finance their activities. The order was given to take the statue and melt it down. The statue was weighed, and was found to weigh only a few grams. It was returned to its place in the Cathedral of Lipari. In reality, the statue weighed many kilograms of silver and it is considered a miracle that it was not melted down.

He was also one of the most adventurous missionaries.

He preached with Philip in Phrygia and Hierapolis; also in Armenia.

He also preached in India, leaving behind a Gospel of Matthew.

After leaving India he went to Greater Armenia where he met a most painful death, he was flayed alive with knives, then crucified head down, like Peter.

It is said that he converted Polymius, the king of Armenia,

To Christianity. Astyages, Polymius' brother, ordered the execution of Bartholomew.

James the Lesser

James, son of Alphaeus, sometimes known as James the lesser to avoid confusion with James son of Zebedee.

He was one of the twelve disciples but little is known about him.

He did write the Epistle of James.

He preached in Palestine and Egypt.

He was put to death by stoning in Jerusalem while he was preaching.

He was stoned by the Jews to whom he was preaching.

But it was also recorded in Acts 12:1, 2, that he was arrested along with some other Christians and executed by Herod Agrippa in 62 AD.

But others say he was crucified in Egypt.

One thing is sure, he died a horrible death.

Judas Escariot

During my research, I couldn't find anything about Judas except relating to his betrayal of Jesus.

He was the son of Simon Escariot who lived in Kerioth in Judah.

Judas was a violent Jewish Nationalist.

Some people believe he betrayed Jesus for the money. Others believe he betrayed Jesus because he had not led the Jews in revolt against the Romans. He was the only disciple who wasn't born in Galilee.

Personally I feel a bit sorry for Judas.

We all know that Jesus was born for one purpose; to be the sacrifice for our sins.

I presume that God's plan was for Jesus to be crucified.

Now if God planned for Jesus to be betrayed in order for him to be sacrificed. Then someone had to betray him.

Judas was the one to do the dirty deed.

After Judas was a broken man, he threw away the coins and eventually hung himself. This happened about 30-33 A D.

But remember if Judas had not betrayed Jesus, then Jesus would not had been crucified and resurrected.

REMEMBER

It was not his betrayal that nailed Jesus to the cross.

It was our Sins

Jude

Jude, was a brother of James the younger. He was one of the little known Apostles and lived in Galilee.

The Epistle of Jude states that it was written by "Jude, a servant of Jesus Christ and brother of James" (Jude 1; 1).

Journeys

He is said to have preached in Judea, Samaria, Idumaea, Syria, Mesopotamia and Libya. He also visited Beirut and Edessa.

He also preached in Assyria and Persia.

Death

It is believed that he was martyred in Beirut, in AD 65.

Together with Simon the Zealot, with who he is normally connected.

They were both beheaded with an axe.

Philip

Philip, was born in Bethsaida, Galilee.

Very little is known about Philip. It is said that he preached in Greece, Syria, and Phrygia.

The thing about Philip was that he was asked in person by Jesus to follow him. (John 1:43).

Philip was martyred in the city of Hierapolis.

Through a miraculous healing and his preaching Philip converted the wife of the Proconsul of the city.

The Proconsul was furious and ordered the torture of Philip, Bartholomew and Marianne.

Philip and Bartholomew were then crucified upside down as was St Peter.

Philip preached from the cross. As a result of his preaching the crowd released Bartholomew from his cross, but Philip insisted that they did not release him.

Philip died in 80 AD.

Simon the Zealot

Simon the Zealot was one of the most obscure of the disciples. Born in Judea, he was the eleventh Apostle chosen by Simon Peter.

He was 28 years old when he became a disciple, and was a fiery agitator.

He was a merchant in Capernaum but turned to the patriotic organization of the zealots.

After the Crucifixion of Jesus, He went into retirement, he was literally crushed.

After a few years he rallied and joined up with Jude as an evangelizing team. He first went to Alexandria and, walked along the Nile, entering into the heart of Africa. He also preached in the Middle East. Christian Ethiopians claim that he was crucified in Samaria, While Justus Lipsius claims that he was sawn in half at Suanir, Persia.

Moses of Chorene writes that he was martyred at Weriosphora in Iberia.

Another tradition says he visited Britain arriving during the Boadicean war 60 AD. Being crucified in 61 AD by the Roman Catus Decianus.

What was certain was that he met a painful death somewhere.

Thomas

Thomas, called Didymus, sometimes called Doubting Thomas because he doubted when first told Jesus was alive.

He was born in the 1st century AD somewhere in Galilee.

After Jesus had risen to Heaven, Thomas sailed to India in AD 52.

He went to tell the good news, landing at the port of Muziris, (modern day North Pavavur) where there was a Jewish community at the time.

The Port was destroyed in 1341 by a massive flood, during the reign of Edward 111 of England.

It is believed that Thomas was killed with Spears at what is known as St Thomas Mount, near Chennai, India in 72 AD.

Matthew

Matthew also called Levi, was possibly born in Galilee.

His father's name was Alpheus and he lived in Capernaum.

His strengths:

- ❖ He was an accurate record keeper.
- ❖ He also knew the Heart of men, and the longings of the Jewish people.
- ❖ He never wavered in serving Jesus.

His weaknesses:

- ❖ Before he met Jesus, he was a very greedy man. He thought that money was the most important thing in life.
- ❖ He was a Tax collector. Tax collectors were often corrupt and often took far more money from the people than what was owed, and kept it extra for themselves. The Roman soldiers backed him so no one objected.

Life Lessons:

God can use anyone to help him in his work.

Don't feel unqualified because of your appearance or education.

Or because of your past.

When Jesus called him, he left his money and followed Jesus.

He was at the Crucifixion of Jesus.

After the Crucifixion he fled and preached in Persia and to the Medes and in Parthia.

He was martyred in Either Ethiopia or Edessa.

Acts

The Book of Acts is Dated around 80-90 AD.

It was written by Luke.

The Acts of the Apostles first used by B Irenaeus.

It is believed that the Book was written as a brief for Theophilus (Thought to be the Lawyer for Paul).

Acts - a three stage structure

> Witness to Christ starts in Jerusalem Chapters 1-7.
>
> To Judea and Samaria 8-10.
>
> Then the Rest of Europe.

Chapter 2, the Day of Pentecost.

The Holy Spirit came on 120 Disciples, at 9am, in Solomon's Porch.

The Gift of tongues and the outpouring, was the reversing of Gods Judgement at the Tower of Babel (Genesis 11).

3000 people responded to Peter's Sermon.

At this time 3000 people was a lot of people.

Luke records at the beginning of chapter 6, how the Gentile Widows complained, about not getting a fair share of the food.

The Apostles were keen to ensure that there was no distinction made between the Jews and Non-Jews.

When it came to Aid, a Jewish/Gentile split had to be avoided.

Stephen's Martyrdom

Stephens's final sermon is one of the longest in the Bible.

(Chapter 7).

It Underlined Luke's purpose of describing how Christianity, changed from being a Jewish National religion, to being a Gentile international faith.

Before the Jewish leaders, Stephen outlined, how Gods activities took place outside their land, before there was a Temple.

That their Accusations, which he was speaking against the Holy Place, and the law, were false, therefore, for God's word and presence, transcend national boundaries.

Philip Went to Samaria and saw many respond to his preaching.

The last time John was in Samaria with Jesus.

He and his Brother James, asked if they could pray that God would send fire from Heaven to burn all the Samarians up.

This was not allowed and now many Samaritans had come to faith.

Philip was transported by God to preach to an Ethiopian Eunuch, on his way home from Jerusalem.

He met him on the Dessert road from Jerusalem to Gaza.

The Eunuch was an important officer, in the service of Candace Queen of Ethiopia.

This is how the Gospel came to Africa.

Paul's Conversion

This is also a pivotal moment (Chapter 9).

This Testimony is recorded 3 times, so that Theophilus might know the evidence given to the other adjudicators.

Once Barnabas and Paul have been sent out at Antioch, the focus of the book moves from Peter to Paul.

Jewish food laws forbad Jews to eat with Gentiles.

Luke then included how GOD, Through Peter.

That eating non-kosher food, was permissible.

ACTS 10

Shows Peter was astonished that the Holy Spirit came upon non-Jews.

CHAPTER 15

Paul was sharing the way his ministry had caused the church to grow.

It is clear that Luke has selected particular events,

In order to show Theophilus , not just the fact that of the churches expansion, but how it took place.

The book of ACTS is the vital link between the Gospels and the Epistles.

While Barnabas was with Paul at Antioch, the followers of Jesus were called Christians for the first Time.

Most of the Books in the New Testament are written by Paul.

But who is Paul?

He is not one of the 12 Apostles.

He is not mentioned in the Gospels.

Without the book of Acts, we would know very little about him, or his ministry.

The Baptism of Believers is another matter of importance of Acts.

Only in Acts is it described as being in water.

Paul frequently refers to Baptism in his letters, but he never links baptism with water.

Baptism in the Holy Spirit occurs in all 4 Gospels, but not saying what is meant.

Acts also helps us when we consider our approach to the laws of Moses today.

The Laws of Moses had 613 Different requirements.

So we need to be clear if we are free, or still binding.

The Answer comes in the great argument, concerning circumcision.

This reached a climax in ACTS 15, when it was settled once and for all.

That Christians are free from the laws of Moses.

Though still bound by the law of Christ.

Even the Word Church, could be misunderstood, were it not for Luke's recording in Acts.

In the Gospels only Matthew mentions the word at all.

In Acts we learn the proper way people are Born Again.

Preaching

When preaching in big cities, Paul would start to Preach in the Synagogue.

When Paul preaches to the Jews, he used the Bible (Old Testament).

But when preaching to the Gentiles, he would try to establish some common ground, before introducing Biblical concepts.

For Example in ACTS 17.

In his message to the Jews, he includes incidents which took place in their past (history), and to poets they knew.

The Tail of the Earthquake and releasing the sheep.

The Alter to the Unknown God.

Paul and Barnabas appointed Elders for each Church.

They Created a Missionary Model.

> 1/ Reaching Key Cities.
>
> 2/ Preaching the Gospel, whilst adapting it to the hearers.
>
> 3/ Making Disciples, rather than decisions.
>
> 4/ Staying with them, and training them.
>
> 5/ Planting Churches, so that they left a community behind.
>
> 6/ Appointing Elders, to lead the communities.
>
> 7/ once a church had local leaders, Apostles should move on.

The Book of Acts was originally called ACTS.

Coming from the Greek Word Praxis, where we get the word Practice.

Therefore Acts describes the practice of Christianity.

The Book is normally called the Acts of the Apostles.

Which is misleading since most of the Apostles don't appear in it.

James is beheaded near the beginning (chapter 12)

John is mentioned beside Peter, but only Peter receives so much space.

Paul gets half the book.

And he was not one of the original twelve.

The Book begins with THE FORMER TREATISE THEOPHILUS.

It was about all that Jesus began to teach and do.

Clearly indicating, what the book was about.

All that Jesus continued doing and teaching.

So it could be called THE ACTS OF JESUS CONTINUES.

The Most prominent person in Acts is the Holy Spirit.

Mentioned 70 times in all.

So maybe it should be called the ACTS of the HOLY SPIRIT.

While the Holy Spirit is mentioned 40 times in the first 13 chapters, God himself is mentioned 100 times.

The Holy Spirit focuses us on Jesus, Jesus focuses us on God.

ACTS is Trinitarian in its Theology.

The Word Trinity is not in the Bible.

But it is short hand expression for the three persons, who make up our GOD

    1/ The Kingdom of God our father.

    2/ the name of Jesus the son.

    3/ the Power of the Holy Spirit.

Conclusion

ACTS is the account of the spread of Christianity.

From Jerusalem to Rome.

Luke sifts the evidence and selects the events which chart this expansion, providing a model for Church life.

Simultaneously he achieves his overall goal of briefing Theophilus, so that his friend Paul, might be found innocent, at his trial.

At the same time God intended that we should understand how he is at work in building his kingdom.

So that whoever we are, and where ever we live.

We might be clear about the ideals, for which we should work and pray.

St Paul

Paul was born between 5 BC and 5 AD.

He was born in the city of Tarsus in South East Turkey.

Tarsus was one of the largest trade centres on the Mediterranean coast.

He was born into a devout Jewish family, but he was also a Roman citizen.

The family had a history of religious piety (Timothy 1:3).

Acts says he became a tent maker.

While he was young, he received an education at the school of Gamaliel, one of the most noted rabbis in history. The Hillel school was noted for giving its students a balanced education, giving Paul broad exposure to classical literature, philosophy, and ethics.

The Bible states very little about Pauls family. Paul's nephew, his sister's son, is mentioned in Acts 23:16. Acts also quotes Paul referring to his father by saying he, Paul, was "a Pharisee, the son of a Pharisee" (Acts 23:6). Paul refers to his mother in Romans 16:13 as among those at Rome.

In Romans 16:7 he states that his relatives, Andronicus and Junia, were Christians before he was and were prominent among the apostles.

He was born with the name Saul.

Popular tradition believes that his name was changed to Paul after meeting Jesus. This is not true as being a Roman citizen he also had a Roman Name (Paul) at birth.

Jesus called him "Saul, Saul "in "the Hebrew tongue" in the book of Acts, when he had the vision which led to his conversion on the road to Damascus.

In Acts 13:9, Saul is called "Paul" for the first time on the island of Cyprus.

Writings

Of the 27 books in the New Testament, 14 have been attributed to Paul; 7 of these are considered authentic and Paul's own, while the authorship of the other 7 are sometimes disputed.

We know through the book of Acts that Paul spoke Hebrew, modern scholars suggests that Koine Greek was his first language.

In his letters he drew on his knowledge of Stoic philosophy, using Stoic terms and metaphors to assist his new Gentile converts in their understanding of the revealed word of God.

Paul or Saul as he was called at the time. Was a devout Jew, who was dedicated to the persecution of the followers of Jesus.

When Stephen was martyred, Saul held the coats of the people who were throwing the stones that killed Stephen.

Saul's Conversion

In the book of Acts, Saul was pursuing a group of followers of Jesus along the road to Damascus, on a mission to bring them back.

While hurrying alone the road, Saul had a vision of the resurrected Jesus. "Saul fell to earth, and heard a voice saying to him, Saul, Saul, why do you persecute me"? "Saul replied "Who are you, Lord? And the Lord said, I am Jesus who you are persecuting.

Jesus appeared in a great light and Saul was blinded.

Some people believe that Saul was blinded by the sun and that he imagined Jesus.

After Saul had got his sight back. He changed totally from being a hater of followers of Jesus, to a totally different man who loved Jesus and on the orders of Jesus he travelled as far as Rome telling everyone about the Good news.

He was beaten, stoned. Ship wrecked and eventually executed.

I don't know about you but if I did what Saul did after having his vision, I would have to be very certain that it was Jesus and not the sun.

Immediately Saul proclaimed Jesus in the Synagogues, saying, and "He is the son of God." And all who heard him were amazed and said, is not this the man who made havoc in Jerusalem of those who called upon his name? And has he not come here for this purpose, to bring him bound before the chief priests? "But Saul increased all the more in strength, and confounded the Jews who lived in Damascus by proving that Jesus was the Christ.

Early Ministry

After Saul's conversion, Saul went to Damascus, where Acts 9 states he was healed of his blindness and baptized by Ananias of Damascus.

Paul says that it was in Damascus that he escaped death.

Paul also says that he then went first to Arabia, and then returned to Damascus. (Gal 1:17)

He may had also been to Mount Sinai (Gal 4: 24-25).

Paul's trip to Arabia is not mentioned anywhere else in the Bible.

Three years after his conversion he went to Jerusalem. There he met James and stayed with Peter for 15 days.

Paul is known for his Missionary Journeys.

First Missionary Journey

At the start of this journey Barnabas was seen as the leader. They went from Antioch to Cyprus then into Asia Minor (Anatolia), and finally returning to Antioch. In Cyprus, Paul rebukes and blinds Elymas the magician who was criticizing their teachings. After this Paul is described as the leader.

They sailed to Perga in Pamphylia. John Mark left them and returned to Jerusalem. Paul and Barnabas go on to Pisidian Antioch.

On the Sabbath they went to the Synagogue. Paul used the occasion to announce a change in his mission which from then on would be to the gentiles.

Let's think about this, The Jews worshiped God.

They believed that one day God would send someone to help them.

Jesus has come and returned to heaven.

So if Jesus was in fact the son of God, Then the Jews would think he was just for them the chosen people.

Here we have Paul telling them that the good news is also for the Gentiles, this now includes me and you.

Many other events happened with Paul before his next Journey, but these I will leave you to look up in your Bible.

Second Missionary Journey

Paul left for his second missionary journey from Jerusalem, in late autumn 49 AD, after the meeting of the council of Jerusalem where circumcision was debated.

On their journey around the Mediterranean Sea, Paul and his companion Barnabas stopped in Antioch where they had an argument about taking John Mark with them on trips.

The Book of Acts said that John Mark had left them on a previous trip and gone home.

Unable to agree on what to do, Paul and Barnabas decided to separate; Barnabas took John Mark with him, while Silas joined Paul.

Paul and Silas visited Tarsus (Paul's birthplace in Eastern Turkey), Derbe and Lystra. In Lystra, they met up with Timothy, a disciple who was spoken well of, and they decided to take him with them.

In Philippi, Paul cast a spirit of divination out of a servant girl, whose masters were not happy about their loss of income her soothsaying provided (Acts 16: 16-24). They set the City against Paul and Silas. They were both put in Jail. After a Miraculous earthquake, the gates of the prison broke, Paul and Silas could had escaped but stayed in the jail.

This event led to the conversion of the jailor (Acts 16: 25-40).

The two Missionaries continued on their travels, going to Berea and then to Athens, where Paul preached to the Jews and God fearing Greeks in the synagogue.

Paul then continued to Corinth.

Corinth

Around 50-52 AD, Paul spent 18 months in Corinth. The Reference in Acts to Proconsul Gallio helps ascertain this date. In Corinth, Paul met Priscilla and Aquila (Acts 18:2) who became faithful followers.

The couple followed Paul to Ephesus, and stayed there to start one of the strongest and most faithful Churches at the time.

In 52 AD, leaving Corinth, Paul stopped at the nearby village of Cenchreae to have his hair cut off, because of a vow he had made earlier. It is possible this was his final haircut before fulfilling his vow to become a Nazirite for a period of time.

With Priscilla and Aquila, the Missionaries then sailed to Ephesus and Paul then went alone to Caesarea to say hallo to the church there. Then he travelled to Antioch, where he stayed for some time, about a year, before leaving on a third journey.

Third Missionary Journey

According to Acts, Paul began his third missionary journey by traveling all around the region of Galatia and Phrygia to strengthen, teach, and rebuke the believers. Paul then travelled to Ephesus, an important centre of early Christianity, and stayed there for almost three years, probably working there as a tentmaker, as he had done when he stayed in Corinth. He performed numerous miracles, healing people and casting out demons, and organized missionary activity in other regions. Paul left

Ephesus after an attack from a local silversmith resulting in a pro-Artemis riot involving most of the city.

During his stay in Ephesus, Paul wrote four letters to the Church of Corinth.

Paul went through Macedonia into Achaea (Acts 20:1-2) and stayed in Greece, probable Corinth, for three months (Acts 20: 1-2) during 56-57 AD. It is believed that Paul dictated his Epistle to the Romans while he was there. He then prepared to travel to Syria, but he changed his mind and travelled back through Macedonia because some Jews had made a plot against him.

In the book of Romans 15: 19 Paul wrote that he visited Illyricum.

On their way back to Jerusalem, Paul and his companions visited Philippi, Troas, Miletus, Rhodes, and Tyre. Paul finished his Journey with a stop in Caesarea, where he and his companions stayed with Philip the Evangelist before finally arriving at Jerusalem.

Rome to Spain

John Chrysostom said that Paul preached in Spain: "for after he had been in Rome, he returned to Spain".

Cyril of Jerusalem said that Paul, "fully preached the Gospel, and instructed even imperial Rome, and carried the earnestness of his preaching as far as Spain.

We have been reading about Paul's Journeys, which he undertook in order to spread the good news but we must not forget that travelling in the time of Paul was a lot different from travelling today.

There was of cause no aeroplanes, Trains, cars, Etc.

If the traveller was lucky they may have a donkey.

To make a long journey you would often have to just walk.

Another problem was that there was often thieves about who would rob and maybe kill you.

On Pauls three missionary journeys he went most of the way by boat. Paul was shipwrecked three times during his journeys.

Jerusalem

In 57 AD Paul made his last visit to Jerusalem, he had brought a collection of money for the local community. Acts reads that he was initially welcomed. However, Acts goes on to recount how Paul was warned by James and the Elders that some of the people were turning against him.

After seven days in Jerusalem, some "Jews from Asia" accused Paul of defiling the temple by bringing Gentiles into it. He was seized and dragged out of the temple by an angry mob. He escaped being killed by surrendering to a group of Roman centurions, who arrested him, they put him in chains and took him to the tribune.

A plot to kill Paul was discovered, so he was transported by night to Caesarea Maritima. He was held in prison for two years, until a new governor suggested he be sent back to Jerusalem for a new trial, Paul then exercised his right as a Roman citizen to "appeal unto Caesar".

Paul was then sent to Rome for trial.

In the book of Acts, it says that on the way to Rome for his appeal to Caesar, Paul was shipwrecked on "Melita" (Malta), the islanders showed him "unusual kindness". From Malta he travelled to Rome.

Rome

Paul arrived in Rome around 60 AD, where he spent two years in house arrest. Paul preached from his rented house for the two years he was held in house arrest awaiting trial.

Death

The date of Paul's death is believed to have occurred after the Great fire of Rome in July 64 AD, but before the last year of Nero's reign, in 68 AD.

Eventually Nero condemned Paul to Death.

As a Roman citizen he was spared Crucifixion and was beheaded.

Jerome in his DE VIRIS ILLUSTRIBUS (198 AD) mentions that "Paul was buried in the Ostian Way at Rome".

Last words - The Beginning

You may think that the title of this final section is unusual.

This book is written as a gateway into reading the Bible.

It is a taster, you have read about ordinary men and women going about their lives, but when God called them, they answered his call and obeyed.

Some enjoyed a great life after completing Gods command, like Joseph.

Others endured a painful death.

We have read about many miracles. We followed the Jews into the Promised Land a journey of 40 years.

We read about prophesies of the prophets, telling us about the birth of a messiah.

In the New Testament We read about the fulfilment of the Prophesies foretold many many years before.

I hope that this book has given you a desire to open your Bible and explore the greatest book ever written.

Amen

PART THREE - DROWNING IN THE HOLY SPIRIT

Drowning in the Holy Spirit

We hear about God and about Jesus,
Also about life after death, and being reborn.
I have been to Church and read the Bible
But is it true what I read and hear, I truly am torn.

Is it enough to believe that God is King of Heaven?
That his Son Jesus died in our place for our sin,
On a Hill far away named Calvary.
Is this all we need to do, to be let in?

To be a true Follower of Jesus Christ,
We need to Drown, not in cold waters.
But To drown in the Holy Spirit, to feel him close to your Skin,
Then open your heart and soul and let him in.

To Drown in the Holy Spirit
Is to be totally filled with the Power of God
No more doubts or sin,
The Holy Spirit now in your body, lives within.

A Gift of Love

O Lord my God, you love me so
Please don't ever, let me go.
You called my name, but I could not hear
I was doing other things, too busy I fear.
Eventually you came down, to look for me.
You searched long, among my dirt and debris
I was heading far away from eternity.

One day my ears finally opened
I heard about a man who died for me,
To save me from hell, he set me free.
He was nailed to a cross, which once was a tree.
He hung there, and for my sins he died
I was so ashamed I cried.

He broke my chains, with that gift of love
My loving Saviour from Heaven above.
He won my heart, with that act of love
My soul had been turning grey,
But I was saved that special day.
He covered my soul, with his pure blood
Now it's his, pure and filled with love.

God's anger

Jonah was a man
Who disobeyed God.
Then ended up
Being swallowed by a fish, like a giant Cod.
God told him to take a message
To a city far away.
He was too scared to go,
So he turned, and ran the other way.
Eventually he took God's message
To the evil city of Nineveh,
And told the king and his people
To repent and sin no more.
He left the city and put up a tent
Then just sat down on the floor,
He waited to see if God would punish,
Or forgive, if they repent.
God does get angry when his people sin
But while his anger simmers
SORRY, can make his Anger Dim.
But when his anger boils
As with Nineveh at another time,
When they felt the wrath,
Of God's Anger boiling over.
The once great city, was destroyed.
Now only Archaeologist dig the ground.
From the people of Nineveh, there is no sound.

My Father in Heaven

I have a father who lives in Heaven, and in my heart.
He is always with me, we're never apart.
In times of trouble, I turn to him.
He gives me a hug and a big grin, then my troubles just disappear,
As though they never did begin.
From the rising of the sun, until the ending of the day,
I chat with my father, it's easy, and all I have to do is pray.
At the sunset of my life,
When the sands in my hourglass are nearly gone.
My father will take me by the hand, saying come along,
Then lead me to Paradise,
Where we can talk together throughout eternity.
My Heavenly father is there for everyone. Bad or nice.
Just call to him and he will answer, that's a certainty.

Thank you

Father God I love you,
You're always by my side.
When I was lost and lonely,
You were my guide.
You climbed down to the debts,
Of my dark despair.
You held my hand and led me out,
My soul you did repair.
You are a kind, loving father,
You forgive me when I repent my wrongs.
You promise eternity in heaven with you, rather,
Than live where there is no music or songs.
How can I ever thank you and show you my love
Through work, money or deeds I would fall.
All that I have is just myself,
Father I give you my life my all.

This one's for you

(Whoever you are)

Close your eyes and start to dream
Look back over your life,
Remember how it's been,
Full of happiness and love?
Or a few blip's along the way,
Which we can leave for another day.

Did you succeed at school?
Pass all your exams
Or not do so well
Sometimes feeling a bit of a fool.

Did you have lots of holidays in the sun?
Some at home others far away,
But where ever you were
I expect they were always fun.

When you get to the autumn of your life
Will you start to think?
How your time on earth will end.
Will you finish as ashes in a pot?
With the Vicar saying, that's your lot.

Maybe there is life after death?
A place to live in total peace
Where anger, wars, and fighting will cease
Will you finish as ashes in a pot?
Or will you explore the possibility
Of living forever in Eternity.

Searching for the star

Three kings many years ago came from afar.
They rode on camels, across mountains and sand
Following a brightness in the sky, a shining star.
Until they found the baby Jesus in a foreign land.

Shepherds were looking after their sheep.
There was no sound in that dark field.
Some shepherds had fallen asleep,
They were woken by a bright Angel, a message he revealed.

Later Kings and Shepherds gathered together in a stable.
A bright Star hovering brightly above,
Mother and father looked down at their baby in the cradle
The prince of peace and the bringer of Hope and Love.

Are you still searching for that star, with the baby underneath?
The star has gone, the baby is a man and no longer small.
He is king of heaven and doesn't ask for costly gifts
Just open your heart and give your all.

A Lesson in Biology

When I was a lad at school,
I loved my science class
What I liked the most I think,
Was the snake they kept under glass.

I learnt about my arms, legs, and head,
My ears, eyes and my Tummy,
We also learnt about internal organs.
Then I would run home to tell my mummy.

Sometimes I went to Sunday school,
But I was left feeling very confused,
When I was told that I had a soul.
I thought the vicar was a bit of a fool
There is no soul in my body,
Only the organs I learnt about at school.

One day when the Vicar was playing the Piano in Church,
He said, sit beside me, and let us talk,
You are wondering about your soul, I hear,
Don't worry others also are confused I fear.

Where is the music coming from, he asked
Inside the Piano, I replied
He then took the Piano apart, piece by piece
Sorry no music inside here he sighed.

The piano produces a sweet sound
But music can only be heard,
Inside the piano no sound will be found.
Your soul is the same, it's there for a start,
Look inside your body, no soul will be found.
But you can feel it in your conscience and your heart.

Have you heard

Have you heard about the man named Jesus?
Who was born many years ago
He was born in Bethlehem,
Which was a long way for his parents to go.

During his short life, he cured the sick
Performed miracles and raised the dead
He walked for miles spreading the good news,
Of forgiveness for Gentiles and Jews

Born in a manger under a star
Shepherds and Kings came from far.
He grew up to be a man who did not sin
Then at 32, the Romans did him in.

He was a good man who did no wrong
But he was tried and although found not guilty
He was nailed to a tree, on a hill called Calvary.
There he died for you and me.

We have all sinned and fallen short
Our punishment will be death in God's court
But God loved us so much, he didn't want us to die
God sent his son to pay for our sins and die in our place
So one day we will meet God face to face.

Fruits of the Spirit - Patience

Patience is a Fruit of the spirit
When someone or something upsets you
Be patient and kind
Stay cool and say "Never mind.

If you start to Anger and lose your cool
God has given you a useful tool.
You have his Gift of Patience and Love
So keep cool and don't be a fool.

God made mankind, then looked down with a big grin
He was Pleased with what he had made.
But man went wrong and started to sin
So he sent a flood, only a few did he save.

This wasn't a lack of Patience,
The Creator wanted to start again.
This new set of people should be ok
The last lot were a real pain.

But again mankind started to sin
God though patiently, what shall I do.
Then again there was that big grin,
I will send my son to die for you.

If God can be patient and cool
When mankind broke his rules
Then how easy it should be for you and me
To be Patient and kind through Eternity.

Footprints

As we journey through our lives,
We leave our footprints along the way.
Were my footprints good, or did I fail?
In the words of the game Monopoly,
Did I pass go, or will I be sent directly to jail.

I hope that I have helped some people
As I travelled along the road of life.
I know I found someone special,
When I met up with my wife.

Since I was a child, I believed in God
But he didn't play a big part in my life.
I was too busy following the desires
Of my body, and my mind.
Jesus seemed too had been left behind.

One evening I went to a local school,
To listen to a preacher talking about Jesus.
That night I felt the Love of God,
But it did not change my life? I was still a fool.

Many years later, the Holy Spirit made his move,
My life changed, I became aware of doing wrongs.
I was able to stop and change my ways.
Now I praise my God by singing songs.

The wish of every Christian parent,
Is for their children to know God.
To be held in his arms and know of his love.
Then eventually to be together in Heaven above.

To follow Jesus is not a time where everything is perfect,
God will not always be seen to answer your prayers.
But he is your Father in Heaven and he will always look after you.
His timing is perfect and his love is always true.

So my children, talk to God in prayer.
He is always there to listen,
And for you he will always care.
I pray that one day you will all the spirit see.
Eventually joining up in Heaven with Jesus and me.

A Child of God

Most days I walk with a spring in my step
In my heart the sky is always blue
God loves me and I love him
Our love is warm and true.

Some days are filled with problems, I start to frown.
God calls to me, and asks,
Why my child are you feeling down?
Remember my spirit is always with you.

Mankind were sinners and heading for hell
God sent his son Jesus to die for us
Now we are redeemed and restored
No longer like a wound filled with pus.

God has set us free, no more condemned.
When people ask, how are you?
Remember you are a child of God,
You are one of the chosen few.

Left Behind - 1 Thessalonians 4:16-17

Years ago, Children went to church on Sundays
We learnt about how God loved us.
At school we had assembles starting on Mondays
We had lessons about Jesus, there was no fuss.

Now religious lessons are multi faith, I know.
On Sundays most people find the shops, a fun place to go
The people that do go to Church are just a few
There are so many other things to do.

Many people only know about Jesus
Through Celebrations in his name.
Christmas, Hot cross buns and Easter Eggs
I guess this now is the name of the game.

Paul writes that Jesus will come again
With the Trumpet call of God,
That the Dead in Christ will rise first, Children, Women and Men.
Those who are left, will be caught up in the clouds
And with Jesus will rise up to heaven, that's so nice
To be with God forever in Paradise.

On that day, many people will be left behind
It doesn't matter if they had been loving and kind.
Or bad and nasty, giving out nothing but hurt.
Taken up will be people whose soul was once filled with dirt,

Who should had been punished, but except Jesus died in their place.
They have repented and are now covered with God's gift of Grace.

We are in the final days, there is not much time left
The evil one may had concealed the truth from you,
But it's not too late, what I have written do not forget.
Read the Bible, learn all about Jesus you can find,
Whatever you do, don't be left behind.

Faith

What do I know about Faith?
The first thing I know is, it's a difficult word to Rhyme.
I think this poem as poems go,
Will take a very long time.

The Dictionaries interpretation of Faith
Is, a strong belief in something,
Without any evidence or proof.
Like when the wind blows tiles off my roof.

I see the faith of a Christian, as a small boat,
Sailing across a wide ocean, to a land far away.
Some days the sea is still and calm,
Other times it's difficult to keep afloat.

At the beginning of our Christian Journey
We are so strong in our Faith.
Then the devil sends doubt into our minds,
Where is God? Sometimes he is so hard to find.

When the good ship us, is sailing in calm water,
Our faith is strong, we have no doubts at all.
But when the waters of our life is like a storm,
The sky becomes overcast, our faith starts to fall.

We must be like the sailors of old
Grab hold of the Mast, and ride out the storm.
But we won't look for a mast to hold,
Call out to Jesus, from his arms you can never be torn.

The Promise of God - Sealed with the blood of Jesus

Eternal life is the promise of God.
We are saved because God made us a Promise,
And that promise is to save those that believe
On Jesus as the Christ the son of God;
What undeserved Love we did receive.

God sent his son Jesus, to die for our sins
He became the offering, for the evil things we had done.
Jesus hung on that Cross, and his blood ran free,
So that we could be forgiven and gain eternity.

Jesus said, I am the way, and the truth, and the life:
No man comes to the father, but by me.
We must all accept the Sacrifice by Jesus that day,
Cover ourselves in his Blood, shed to set us free.

Broken Chains

As I wandered through my life
A veil seemed to cover my eyes
I was in darkness I could not see
Youthful passions were consuming me
My spirit was willing
But my flesh was weak
Then Jesus came down my soul to seek
He covered me in love
And forgave my sins
Then broke my chains
And set me free
I am no longer condemned
It's Eternity for me.

A Letter to God

Dear God,
King of Kings, The only true God.
My Father who lives in Heaven.
Take my Love, take my Life too,
I just can't stop loving you.

Through your Deity, you sent your son,
To die, as a sacrifice for my sin.
So I will be found not guilty, on Judgement day,
And St Peter will wave and say "let him in."

Your Holy Spirit is always by my side,
If I am tempted or going wrong,
He will protect me and be my guide.
I will always march, to your song.

When my number is up,
And my time has finally come.
You will hold my hand, and lead me on,
To Paradise and your world beyond.
Yours Forever
Your Loving son.

Walking with God

There has been times in my life when I wandered
Following the desire of my body and my mind
I was lost condemned by my sins
Then Jesus came down my soul to find.

The Father sent Jesus to be nailed to a cross
Made from the wood of a nearby tree
There he hung and suffered pain
So my sins would be forgiven, and I would be set free.

What does God now require of me?
The Bible tells us in the book of Micah
To act justly, love mercy and to walk humbly
With the Lord our God.

Then in heaven we will live throughout eternity.

Psalm 151

During my life I have had many loves,
But one love is above them all.
This love is always with me, through,
The spring, the summer and the fall.
I will always love my wife,
My love for her has blossomed,
Into the most fragrant rose in the garden,
She is the love of my life.
I have had a love for football for many years
But compared to my love for God,
Everything else just fades away.
I will love my God, for ever and a day.
The love of God, is like no other love.
When I truly repent of the wrongs I have done,
He forgives me, then unlike myself, he forgets them,
My sins are then listed as none.
2000 years ago, my God performed
The greatest act of love there has ever been.
He sent his beloved son,
To be nailed to a cross, to suffer and die.
As a sacrifice for my sin,
So one day, I can share paradise with him.

Printed in Great Britain
by Amazon